HOW TO DO
just about
ANYTHING IN
Microsoft®
Excel

D1364683

ELMVALE

READER'S DIGEST

HOW TO DO
just about
ANYTHING IN
Microsoft®
Excel

Published by The Reader's Digest Association Limited
London • New York • Sydney • Montreal

How to do just about anything in Microsoft® Excel

was edited and designed by The Reader's Digest Association Limited, London

First edition Copyright ©2003
The Reader's Digest Association Limited,
11 Westferry Circus, Canary Wharf, London E14 4HE.
www.readersdigest.co.uk

Printed in Hong Kong

ISBN 0 276 42612 6
Book Code 400-188-02

PLANET THREE PUBLISHING NETWORK

Edited, designed and produced by
Planet Three Publishing Network
Northburgh House, 10 Northburgh Street,
London EC1V 0AT

Editor
Kevin Wiltshire

Sub Editor
Emily Kerry

Art Editor
Susan Gooding

Designer
Yuen Ching Lam

Authenticator
Tony Rilett

For Reader's Digest
Editor
Caroline Boucher
Art Editor
Julie Bennett

Reader's Digest General Books
Editorial Director
Cortina Butler
Art Director
Nick Clark
Executive Editor
Julian Browne
Managing Editor
Alastair Holmes
Style Editor
Ron Pankhurst

Contents

Using Graphics

Customising Excel

Displaying Your Data

Excel's Advanced Features

How to use this book

The clear instructions and useful projects in this book guide you step by step through Excel's main features. Each stage is illustrated with pictures showing you what you will see on screen, and important items, buttons and menu commands are highlighted in bold text. With just a little practice, you'll soon be using spreadsheets with ease, both at home and at work.

GETTING AROUND THE BOOK

The seven chapters in this book cover Excel's most useful features, starting with the basics and gradually moving on to more advanced tasks.

Basics
Learn how to enter data and work with simple formulas. This chapter also includes sections on saving and printing your spreadsheet.

Editing your worksheet
Once you've created your first spreadsheet you'll soon want to copy and move data around, and you might want to add comments or information that prints on every page.

Formatting your worksheet
It's important to tell Excel what type of data you are entering, so that it can work with the information correctly. You can also style your data to improve legibility by changing the colour of cells and text, and applying borders.

Using graphics
Excel allows you to present your data in the form of a chart so the information is easier to analyse. You can also jazz up your spreadsheets by using WordArt and inserting images.

Displaying your data
Excel gives you complete control over the way your data is presented. You can sort it by date or alphabetically, choose to hide certain rows and columns, or freeze particular data so it always remains visible on screen.

Customising Excel
Find out how to change the way Excel works and looks to suit your individual preferences.

Excel's advanced features
Excel has many built-in functions, which can make the most complex calculations effortless. This chapter shows you how to use them.

WHICH VERSION OF EXCEL
The information in this book is based on a PC using Excel 2002 (part of the Office XP suite of programs) and Windows XP Home edition. You can upgrade your PC from an earlier version of Office or install the Office suite from scratch. Either task is made easy using wizards.

Close up
These project-related tips offer you extra detail on various Excel functions.

Bright idea
Wondering how to use your new-found skills? Look out for these tips.

Key word
You'll find handy definitions of technical words or phrases here.

GETTING AROUND THE PAGE

Acquaint yourself with the key visual features that appear throughout the book to help you work through each task.

See also
These are cross references to other pages containing related information.

Step-by-step
Projects are set out in easy-to-follow steps with accompanying snapshots.

Useful tips
Find tips, tricks and the solutions to common problems above or below the numbered steps.

Before you start
Step-by-step projects begin with a short section of text. This outlines important points and any necessary preparatory work.

Snapshots
Each step is illustrated with images showing exactly what you'll see on your screen.

Enclosed sections
Important menus, buttons or key sections of the screen are highlighted so you can locate them easily.

Type in quotes
Words enclosed by quotation marks show the exact words you will see on screen, or indicate what you need to type in as part of a step.

EDITING YOUR WORKSHEET

Columns and rows

Excel's grid-like structure of columns and rows makes it ideal for storing and presenting data. You can easily change the width of a column and the height of a row just by clicking and dragging. Excel also keeps track of your formulas and formatting so that inserting a row or a column doesn't change your calculations or cause problems with spreadsheet design.

BEFORE YOU START
Enter some sample text and spreadsheet. You will need to numbers in several columns. make text entries wider

SEE ALSO...
● Format your data p 42
● Aligning data p 46

Expert advice
If you want to change the width of several columns in one go, select the columns by clicking on the first column letter and then dragging your mouse pointer to the last letter. Drag the boundary between any two of the selected columns' letter headings to widen all the columns at the same time. This same principle can be applied to rows.

Watch out
If you have entered a column of data and want to make it narrower, check that you don't cause items further down the page to overflow their cells. If you are unsure, click on the column heading letter to select the whole column, and then click on the **Format** menu, choose **Column** and click on **AutoFit Selection**. This reduces the width to fit the largest item on the list.

1 In our example above, we have entered the column headings in Excel's default font size. However, 'Description' is too long to fit in its column. To make column C wider, move the mouse pointer over the boundary between the 'C'

1 To sort your new database of birthdays by date, click anywhere in the column of dates to select a single cell. Then click on the **Data** menu and choose **Sort**. When the **Sort** dialogue box opens, make sure the 'Header row' option under **My list has** is selected. Excel automatically selects your 'Birthday' column under **Sort by**.

3 Excel automatically increases the height of rows if you increase the size of the font you are using (see page 44). However, you may want to increase the height of a row yourself to add a little space, for example, between the spreadsheet title and the column headings. Click on the boundary between row number headings, in this case rows '2' and '3', and drag it downwards. This will increase the height of row 2 to create a little more space above the column headings. Again, a pop-up box displays the height as you drag.

4 If you want to set all the columns in a new spreadsheet to a standard width, click on the **Format** menu, choose **Column** and then select **Standard Width**. Excel's default column width is 6.43. Type in whatever value you require – in our example we have chosen '11' – and click on the **OK** button. All the columns will now be set to the selected width. Note that, if you have previously adjusted the width of a column, it will not be affected by this action.

Bold type
All buttons, menu items, keys, dialogue box names and tabs, and important Excel features are shown in bold text.

Page turns
A green arrow in the bottom right corner of a page indicates that the project continues over the page.

That's amazing!
You can enhance the way you work with Excel using these inspiring ideas, explanations and items of special interest.

Watch out
These tips warn you of possible difficulties and pitfalls when using Excel, and give helpful advice on how to avoid problems.

Expert advice
Advanced tips offer guidance on specific features and useful advice on how to get professional results with Excel.

Set up your PC safely

When you are choosing a suitable location for your PC, check that there is enough space for all the equipment and an adequate number of mains sockets. You need to consider lighting and seating, and the surface area of your desk. If you want to connect to the Internet or send faxes from your computer, you will also need to be near a telephone socket.

SITTING AT YOUR COMPUTER

You need to think carefully about how to arrange your work area, as a poorly laid out computer desk and PC will be tiring to use and may prevent you from operating your PC properly.

If you find yourself leaning towards the monitor, increase the zoom level at which you are viewing your document.

Your legs should remain uncrossed and your knees should be lower than your hips.

An adjustable chair will support your back and can be altered to suit each family user.

The monitor should be around 50cm from your eyes.

Your desk should be a comfortable height for typing, with your upper arms parallel to your body and your lower arms parallel to the floor.

Your feet should rest flat on the floor.

NAMING AND PLACING PARTS

Your PC's hardware includes all the parts that you can actually see and handle. Knowing how to position these elements ensures a safe and efficient work area.

System unit
This is the part of your computer to which everything is connected. Leave space so that you can plug in the cables easily and to allow for ventilation. Don't leave cables trailing.

Monitor
This is the computer's screen. Position your monitor to avoid reflections, but do not face a bright window yourself as this may lead to eyestrain.

Speakers
For the best sound quality, speakers should be well spaced apart on either side of the monitor and at desk level or higher, not just pushed under the desk.

Printer
Position your printer near the system unit. Make sure there is sufficient space around it for loading the paper trays.

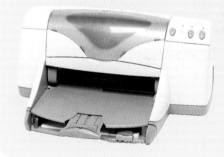

Keyboard
Make sure the keyboard is on a stable and level surface within easy reach. Leave enough space in front of it for hands and wrists. Ensure that the desk is at the correct height.

Mouse
Place the mouse to the side of your keyboard that suits whether you are left- or right-handed. Use a mouse mat to create the correct amount of friction, and be sure there is plenty of room to move the mouse around.

Expert advice
If you are planning to use your computer for long periods, either surfing the Internet or doing your accounts and letters, then you should invest in a good-quality comfortable office chair. Most dining chairs do not offer the support for your back that is vitally important when you are sitting still for long periods. Also, most office chairs are adjustable and so will suit every member of the family. Remember, even with a comfortable chair, you should take regular 10 minute breaks to walk around.

What is Excel?

Excel is a program that creates spreadsheets. A spreadsheet consists of a grid of cells, arranged in columns and rows, which can contain numbers, formulas or text. You can use spreadsheets to do almost anything, from calculating and analysing your personal and business accounts, to logically storing and sorting lists of addresses or everyday items.

Close up
Excel calls its spreadsheets 'worksheets'. An Excel file is called a workbook and can contain multiple worksheets, accessed by clicking tabs at the bottom of the screen.

WHAT YOU CAN DO

An Excel spreadsheet enables you to organise numerical data, to perform calculations and to present the results in a logical and clear format. As well as calculating values, you can also use Excel to manage lists of information.

Perform calculations

Excel is a powerful calculating tool – once you've entered your data, you can create formulas to instruct the spreadsheet to take the values from specified cells, perform a calculation and then display the answer. Excel contains hundreds of built-in formulas, called functions, which can help you do anything from totalling a column of figures to analysing a company's staff costs over a five-year period. Even the most sophisticated Excel spreadsheets use the basic mathematical operators – plus, minus, multiply, divide and equals – to perform their calculations.

A3	▼	f_x =A1+A2	
	A	B	C
1	2		
2	3		
3	5		
4			

Store your data

Excel can handle text as well as numbers, and is an excellent means of storing and organising information, such as a list of club members or an inventory of your home contents. It has lots of useful features to help you enter and view your data quickly and easily, and to present the information in a clear, informative way. You can sort lists alphabetically, filter the contents of a list so that only certain items are visible, or even use Excel's built-in functions (see left) to automatically count how many items in a list match the specified criteria.

Choose a style

Once you have entered your data, it makes sense to style your column and row headings as well as the results of the calculations so that they stand out. Excel includes familiar tools that are common to the Microsoft Office Suite of programs, such as fonts (typefaces), styles, colours and borders. You can even format each cell individually to draw the reader's eye to important items.

Design your page

Like a word processor document, spreadsheets can be formatted to suit your needs. There are options to align text, add headers and footers and modify page shape and size. And there's also a useful feature to make sure all the selected information fits onto the page. Excel has access to the Office Clip Art resources and you can add pictures and WordArt to spreadsheets to illustrate your information. If you would like to display your data in a pictorial form, you can choose from a range of colourful two and three-dimensional graphs using the **Chart Wizard**.

Automatic support

If you need help with using Excel, the **Office Assistant** can answer questions, and **Smart Tags** and buttons pop up to give you context-sensitive guidance and shortcuts while you work – these may provide links to a Web site for further information.

The Task Pane

At the right-hand side of Excel's window, a panel is displayed that offers quick and easy access to a range of commonly used commands. You can use it to open files you've recently worked on, access templates, search for documents or text, manage your Office Clipboard and look for Clip Art.

THE SPREADSHEET WINDOW

Depending on whether you upgraded or installed Office, Excel's toolbars may take up one or two rows. To see all the buttons (as shown below), click on the down arrow at the right of any toolbar and choose 'Show Buttons on Two Rows'.

Title bar
Shows the title of the spreadsheet document on which you are currently working.

Menu bar
Contains drop-down lists of commands, arranged by category.

Standard toolbar
Single-click buttons activate the most common commands.

Formatting toolbar
Buttons and drop-down menus are used for formatting data and cells.

Name box
The co-ordinates (column letter and row number) of the selected cell are indicated here. You can use this box to name sections of your sheet for easier navigation and printing.

Selected cell
A black border indicates the selected cell.

Row headers
These numbers identify each row. Using a combination of a column letter and a row number, each cell is given a unique address.

Worksheet tabs
These tabs allow the user to switch between worksheets. Right-click on a tab to insert, remove, rename or move worksheets.

Windows Taskbar
Contains the Start button and some useful shortcuts to your programs and settings.

Column headers
Each column is identified by a letter, or letters.

Mouse pointer
When the mouse pointer becomes a cross, you can select cells or drag items.

Formula Bar
The contents of the selected cell are displayed here for editing.

Scroll bars
Use the arrows to move slowly around the spreadsheet. Drag the scroll boxes to move quickly up and down or from left to right.

Close buttons
The red cross button closes Excel. The cross underneath closes the spreadsheet window.

Maximize/Restore Down button
If this button displays a square, clicking on it will cause the Excel window to fill your screen. If the button contains two overlapping squares, clicking on it will shrink the window.

Minimize button
Click here to reduce the Excel window to a button on the Taskbar. Click on this button to restore the window.

Task Pane
This may display one of four panels containing quick links to documents and templates, the Clipboard, Clip Art and search tools.

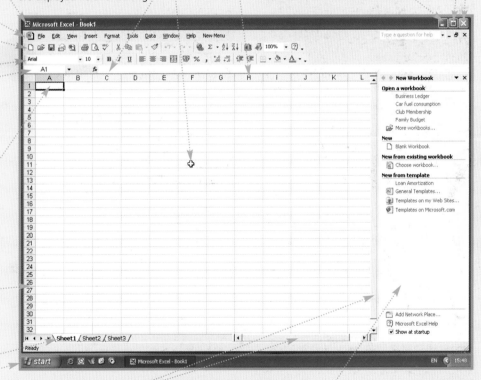

USING THE KEYBOARD

Function keys are shortcuts to commands:
F1 accesses **Microsoft Help and Support**.
F2 is for editing data either in a cell or on the **Formula Bar**: select a cell and press **F2**, use the mouse or arrow keys to position the insertion point and then edit the cell's contents.

F4 repeats your last command.
F5 opens a **Go To** dialogue box, which enables you to jump to another part of your document.
F7 checks a document for spelling.
F11 inserts a chart using the selected data.
F12 opens the **Save As** dialogue box.

Delete gets rid of any selected data or item.
Home takes you to column A.
End plus any arrow key moves in the selected direction to the last cell in your data range.
Page Up moves up one screen at a time.
Page Down moves down one screen at a time.

Tab moves you one cell to the right.
Caps Lock makes all the letters that you type appear as capitals.
Shift allows you to type a letter as a capital or to select the top-marked option on a key. For example, pressing **Shift + 5** types the **%** symbol.
Ctrl and **Alt** keys, when pressed separately in conjunction with other keys, provide quick access to certain commands. For example, **Ctrl + P** displays the **Print** dialogue box.
Windows key accesses the **Start** menu.

Spacebar adds spaces between words.
Return key confirms any data you have entered in a cell.
Backspace deletes text to the left of your cursor.

Arrow (cursor) keys navigate up, down, left and right to adjacent cells.
Enter key works like the **Return** key.

Keyboard shortcuts

You can use all kinds of shortcuts to style your data and format your spreadsheets:

Ctrl + Home moves you to cell A1.
Ctrl + B makes data in the selected cell(s) bold.
Ctrl + U underlines data.
Ctrl + I italicises data.
Ctrl + A selects the entire spreadsheet.
Ctrl + Z undoes the last action.
Ctrl + Y repeats the last action.
Ctrl + Spacebar selects the entire column.

Shift + Spacebar selects the entire row.
Shift + F5 displays the **Find** dialogue box.
Shift + F2 edits a comment.
Shift + Tab confirms a cell entry and moves one cell to the left.

Alt + F4 closes the Excel program.
Alt + F8 runs a pre-recorded macro.
Alt + Return starts a new line in a cell.

Close up
Use the Help *menu to find out more about Excel's function keys and shortcuts using* Alt *and* Ctrl. *Click the question mark icon on the toolbar and type in 'keyboard shortcuts'. Click* Search.

Basics

Explore the program

Excel's menus and toolbars are designed to be similar to other Microsoft Office programs so if you've used Word before you'll instantly recognise the common elements and familiar tools. Even if you haven't used another Office program, Excel's menus are logically laid out and, with a little practice, you'll soon familiarise yourself with its built-in tools and features.

SEE ALSO...
● *What is Excel?* *p 12*
● *Change menus and toolbars* *p 84*

BEFORE YOU START
If your toolbars occupy only one row instead of two, click on the *down-arrow at the right of any toolbar and choose 'Show Buttons on Two Rows' from the menu.*

1 To launch Excel, click on the **Start** button – visible at the bottom left of your screen – and then click on **All Programs**. Move the mouse pointer across to highlight **Microsoft Excel** and click once.

2 While the program data is being loaded into memory from the hard disk, you will see a splash screen. This is a small window that tells you which version of Excel you are using and to whom it is registered.

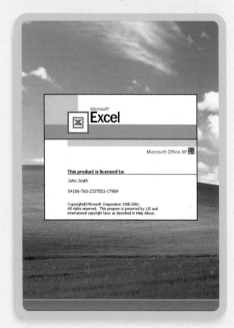

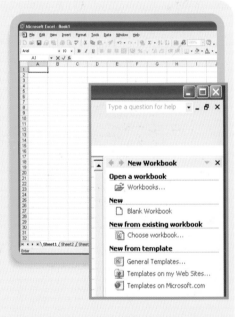

3 When Excel has finished loading, a new blank document opens. At the top are the menus and toolbars, to the right and at the bottom of the grid are the scroll bars, and the **New Workbook** panel of the **Task Pane** occupies the right of the screen.

GETTING AROUND IN EXCEL

If you are not familiar with spreadsheets, it's a good idea to acquaint yourself with the basic features before you get started.

Using the mouse

The mouse is the primary tool for clicking on, moving and selecting items in Excel. It should be used on a mouse mat and orientated with its 'tail' pointing towards the screen. When following the instructions in this book, 'click' means to single-click on the left mouse button; 'right-click' indicates that you should use the right mouse button.

The pointer in Excel is an outlined cross (see left, top). This enables you to select a cell or range of cells. When you are entering or editing text, the pointer changes to a tall capital I (see left, centre). Clicking with this pointer positions the insertion point, a flashing vertical bar, ready for new text to be entered. When you move the mouse pointer over the menus and toolbars, it turns into the familiar Windows arrow (see left, bottom). Use this to click on items.

Selecting cells

Excel always opens with the top left cell selected in a new blank spreadsheet. This cell is called A1 because the cell is at the intersection of column A and row 1. All the cells on a spreadsheet have a unique reference, which is derived from their column letter and row number. You can see the reference for the currently selected cell in the **Name Box**, to the left of the **Formula**

Bar. The currently selected cell has a dark black outline. To enter text in it, just start typing. To move to (select) another cell, position the cross-shaped mouse pointer over it, click once and start typing. It is also possible to move to another cell by using the keyboard arrow keys.

To select a range of cells – A3 to F20, for example – click on A3 and hold down the mouse button. Then drag the mouse to the right and down to cell F20. The cells will be highlighted. If the range is larger than the window, select the top left cell in the range, hold down the **Shift** key on your keyboard, then move down the spreadsheet using the scroll bars until the bottom right cell in the range is visible and click once on that cell.

Moving around a spreadsheet

A spreadsheet is a vast grid of cells stretching across and down the screen – there are 65536 rows and 256 columns, making nearly 17 million cells – so it is easy to get lost. Pressing the **Ctrl** and **Home** keys together takes you back to cell A1. Alternatively, you can click on the **Edit** menu and choose **Go To**, then type A1 and press the **Return** key. You can use the horizontal and vertical scroll bars to move around the page by clicking on the arrows at either end of the scroll bars, by dragging the box up and down, or by clicking on the small bar above or below the box to move up or down a screen at a time.

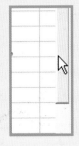

Menus, toolbars and commands

There are three ways to give Excel instructions: menus, toolbars or shortcut keys. The menus are at the top of the window and include commands for editing, saving and printing your work. Click once on a menu item to bring up a list, move the mouse pointer down the list and click again on an item to select it. Many of the menu commands are duplicated on the toolbar for quick access. For instance, you can undo your last action by clicking on the **Edit** menu and choosing **Undo**. However, you can perform

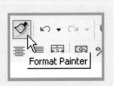

this action more quickly by clicking on the **Undo** button. Other buttons offer quick routes to formatting and saving options. If you are unsure what a button does, hover the mouse pointer over it and a helpful **ToolTip** pops up.

When you open a drop-down menu, you will see some text next to each item. For instance, **Ctrl+C** is next to **Copy**. This means that item has an equivalent keyboard shortcut. To copy a cell's contents using this shortcut, select the cell, hold down the **Ctrl** key at the bottom left of your keyboard and press **C**.

THE MENU BAR

All of Excel's features and tools can be found on the drop-down menus under the headings on the Menu bar.

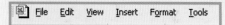

Try clicking on each menu item in turn to familiarise yourself with the contents of the drop-down menus. Some menu items have an icon next to them, representing the corresponding button on the toolbar. There are also keyboard shortcuts next to some items. You can use these if you prefer not to use the menus and buttons.

File

Items in the **File** menu refer to the management of spreadsheet documents, and include commands such as **Save** and **Print**. Click on **New** to create a blank spreadsheet and on **Open** to load a previously saved spreadsheet.

Edit

Commands on the **Edit** menu enable you to cut, copy, paste and delete items. There's also a useful search function and an **Undo** command that reverses your actions one at a time if something goes wrong.

View

The **View** menu contains options to change the way you see the spreadsheet on screen and to add and remove toolbars.

Insert

This menu includes features that enable the user to add rows and columns to a spreadsheet, insert a 'Function' (or formula), and to start the **Chart Wizard** to help you create a graph.

Format

If you want to change the way a cell or its contents look, use the **Format** menu. It includes commands to hide individual rows and columns and to protect cells from being edited.

Tools

On the **Tools** menu you can find specialist features, such as spell-checking, speech and **AutoCorrect** options. You'll also find a feature for password-protecting the worksheet.

Data

The **Data** menu includes some of Excel's most powerful functions. You can sort your data, filter it so you can only see certain items, and group rows and columns so you can hide or reveal them with a single click.

Window

Commands on the **Window** menu allow you to organise multiple spreadsheets on your screen so you can switch between them or see them all at once.

Help

If you need help with any aspect of Excel, click on **Microsoft Excel Help** to see the **Office Assistant**, and type a question. For help with an on-screen item, click on **Help** and choose **What's This?**. Now when you click on the item, a small box will appear describing the function of that item.

Full menus

By default, Excel only displays basic commands and frequently used items on each menu. The full menu can be viewed by clicking the downward-pointing double arrow at the bottom of the menu. If you want all the options on a menu to be visible when you click on it, right-click on a toolbar, choose **Customize** and click on the **Options** tab. Put a tick next to 'Always show full menus'.

Close up
A downward-pointing double arrow at the bottom of a drop-down menu means there are more options available on that menu. A small right arrow next to an item indicates that more items are contained in a sub-menu. Click on the arrows to see the extra items.

THE STANDARD TOOLBAR

This is positioned directly under the Menu bar at the top left of the screen.

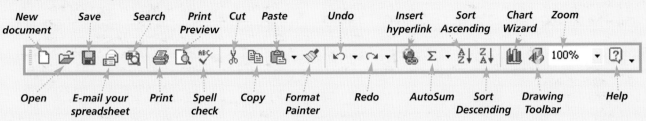

New document • Save • Search • Print Preview • Cut • Paste • Undo • Insert hyperlink • Sort Ascending • Chart Wizard • Zoom

Open • E-mail your spreadsheet • Print • Spell check • Copy • Format Painter • Redo • AutoSum • Sort Descending • Drawing Toolbar • Help

THE FORMATTING TOOLBAR

This may be on the same row as the Standard toolbar – follow the instructions on page 16 to place it on its own row.

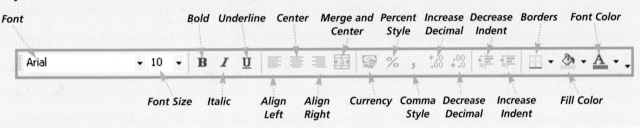

Font • Bold • Underline • Center • Merge and Center • Percent Style • Increase Decimal • Decrease Indent • Borders • Font Color

Font Size • Italic • Align Left • Align Right • Currency • Comma Style • Decrease Decimal • Increase Indent • Fill Color

THE TASK PANE

This panel provides quick access to routine commands, such as opening files and inserting Clip Art.

Under **New Workbook** you can choose from a list of recently saved files, or create a new workbook.

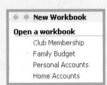

The **Clipboard** displays the last 24 copied or cut items. Select the cell into which you want to insert the copy and then click an item on the **Clipboard**.

You can use **Search** to find files or text in any Office file on your PC.

Office is supplied with Clip Art, a collection of illustrations and pictures, categorised by theme and keywords. You can search for images by entering keywords into this panel.

Expert advice
To quickly add or remove buttons from a toolbar, click on the small downward arrow at the far right end of the bar. Choose 'Add or Remove Buttons' and then select the toolbar you are working on. Use the tick boxes to choose which buttons to add or remove.

Bright idea
Use the Undo *button to go back if you make a mistake. Click on the downward arrow next to the button to see a drop-down list of actions to help you jump back several steps. Unlike Word, Excel empties the list each time you save.*

Entering data

Getting your information into Excel is simple – just click on a cell anywhere on your spreadsheet and start typing. Then select another cell or press the Return key to confirm the data. If you need to edit your data, either make the changes in the cell, or type them in the Formula Bar. You can move around using the keyboard arrow keys or by clicking with the mouse.

SEE ALSO...
- *What is Excel?* p 12
- *Explore the program* p 16
- *Excel formulas* p 24

BEFORE YOU START
Have all the information that you might want to enter into your *spreadsheet to hand. Don't worry about organising it, as Excel can do that for you afterwards.*

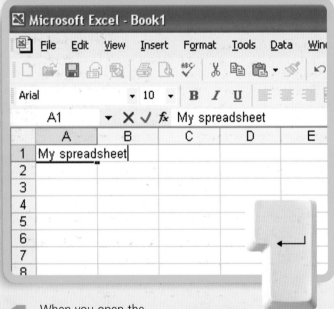

1 When you open the Excel program, cell A1 is always selected in the top-left corner of a blank spreadsheet. You can type the title of your spreadsheet straight into this cell, or select another one by clicking on it. When you've finished typing, press **Return** or click on another cell. You can also select cells by using the keyboard arrow keys.

2 As a rule, keep row 1 empty except for your title and start entering your data a few rows down. Press the **Down** arrow key on your keyboard a few times to move down, or click on a cell with your mouse, and start typing. Use the **Right** arrow or the **Tab** key on your computer keyboard to move across the row to enter your column headings.

Undoing mistakes

If you start typing in a cell that already contains some data, you will replace that data with whatever you type. If you accidentally delete the contents of a cell, press the **Esc** key or click the **Cancel** button on the **Formula Bar** to restore them. If you have moved away from the cell or pressed **Return**, use the **Undo** button to reverse your actions one step at a time.

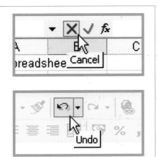

Close up
If you are entering a lot of data arranged in rows, use the Tab *key to move to the right. When you press* Return *at the end of a row, Excel will automatically move you to the beginning of the next row down.*

4 To edit the contents of a cell, you can either double-click on the cell, or select it and click on its text in the **Formula Bar** (below). If you can't edit a cell by double-clicking on it, go to the **Tools** menu and choose **Options**. Then click on the **Edit** tab, put a tick next to 'Edit directly in cell' and click on **OK**. Position the insertion point (the flashing vertical bar) by clicking with the mouse, and use the **Backspace** key (above left) to delete text before the insertion point and the **Delete** key to delete text after the insertion point. If you want to replace the entire contents of a cell, just select it and start typing.

3 Use the **Shift** key to type a capital letter and to select the symbols on the upper portion of the punctuation and number keys. Don't use the mathematical operator symbols – plus **(+)**, minus **(-)**, multiply **(*)**, divide **(/)** and equals **(=)** – unless you are entering a formula (see page 24) or a date (see page 94). Otherwise Excel will display the '#NAME?' error message.

Save your work

When you save a spreadsheet, its digital data is copied from the computer's memory to the hard disk drive, where it is stored until you next open the file. If you don't save your work, all the data will be lost when you exit the program or switch off your PC. Remember to save regularly so you don't lose important work if your computer crashes.

SEE ALSO...
● *Entering data* p 20

BEFORE YOU START
To save a spreadsheet for the first time, click on the **File** menu and choose **Save**. You can also click the **Save** button on the toolbar, or press **Ctrl** and **S** on the keyboard.

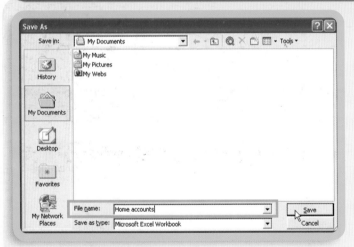

2 Although the **My Documents** folder is a good place to store your spreadsheets, it can become cluttered, making files difficult to locate. Choose a different location from the **Places Bar** buttons on the left of the window. Alternatively, create your own new folder. Click on the **Create New Folder** button, type an appropriate name for your folder and click on the **OK** button. Excel creates your folder and changes the folder in the **Save in** box to your new folder name.

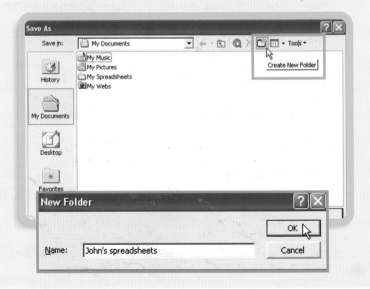

1 The first time you save a file, the **Save As** dialogue box appears because the file does not yet have a name or destination folder on your hard disk. Type a recognisable file name for your spreadsheet in the **File name** box – you can use up to 256 characters including spaces, but you can't use symbols such as **?** and *****. Excel chooses **My Documents** as the default location for your file, so this location is selected in the **Save in** box.

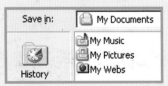

Watch out

Once you have saved your spreadsheet, if you want to save any subsequent changes to the document, choose **Save** from the **File** menu. However, if you have edited the spreadsheet and want to save it as a different version of the current document, choose **Save As** from the **File** menu to make a new file. Otherwise you will save over your previous work.

The Places Bar

Use the buttons on the **Places Bar** to quickly switch to another location on your hard disk. Just click once on a button to open its folder. You can add a favourite folder to the bar by selecting the required folder in the **Save As** box, clicking on **Tools** and choosing 'Add to "My Places"'.

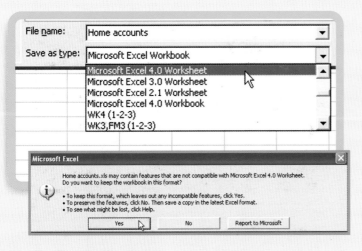

3 Under the **File name** box is a drop-down list called **Save as type**. This enables you to save files in different formats. This box should be left as 'Microsoft Excel Workbook' unless you are saving a file for someone with an older version of Excel, or someone who uses a different spreadsheet program, such as Microsoft Works or Lotus 1-2-3. Scroll down the **Save as type** list to see all the options. If you choose a different file type, you may see a message appear, warning that some advanced features not compatible with other spreadsheets will be lost. Click on the **Yes** button if you want to go ahead with the save.

4 When you are happy with your file name, folder and file type, click on the **Save** button. The **Save As** dialogue box closes and the file name is displayed in the **Title bar** at the top of the window. To save as you work, you can press **Ctrl + S** or click on the **Save** button on the Standard toolbar.

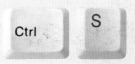

Excel formulas

Each cell in an Excel spreadsheet has its own address, made up of its column and row references. This means that a calculation in one cell can refer to other cells – for instance, A1 could display the result of A2 + A3. In fact, using just the simple mathematical operators – plus, minus, multiply and divide – you can build an extremely useful spreadsheet.

SEE ALSO...
- *Using AutoSum* p 26
- *Cut, copy and paste* p 32
- *Advanced functions* p 90

BEFORE YOU START
Create a new spreadsheet and carefully copy the column headings illustrated in Step 1 below. Enter some of your monthly shopping items, prices and amounts.

1 Once you have entered some data into your spreadsheet you can perform some calculations on the values in the cells. Click in cell E4 under 'Total' and type '='. This tells Excel you are about to enter a formula. Then click on C4 under 'Price', type '*' (**Shift + 8** on the keyboard), click on D4 under 'Amount' and press **Return**.

2 The formula '=C4*D4' in cell E4 tells Excel to multiply the contents of C4 by the contents of D4 and display the result in E4, which in this case is 7. Excel will recalculate this value every time you change a value in C4 or D4. Try changing the value in cell C4 to '2' and the value in cell D4 to '5' – the total in E4 will change automatically each time you enter a new number.

3 Change the price and amount back to the original values and move to cell E5. Instead of clicking to select the cells to be used in the calculation you can enter them directly, so type in '=C5*D5' and press **Return**. The result will then appear. Continue to add formulas until you get to the end of your list.

Copying formulas

A quick way of copying a formula to an adjacent cell is to use the **Fill Handle**: move the mouse pointer over the small black square in the bottom right corner of the selected cell and the pointer will change to a black **+** sign. Click and drag it to an adjacent cell where you want the formula to be pasted and release the mouse button.

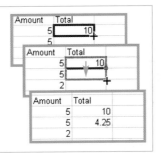

Amount	Total
5	10
5	

Amount	Total
5	10
5	
2	

Amount	Total
5	10
5	4.25
2	

Watch out

When constructing formulas that involve multiplication and division as well as addition and subtraction, make sure you bear in mind the 'order of operations' – multiplication and division must be completed before addition and subtraction. If you want to create a formula that adds two numbers together before multiplying them by a third number, you must enclose the addition in brackets because Excel performs the calculation in brackets first. For example, '=(3+4)*2'.

	A	B	C	D	E
1	Monthly Shopping Budget				
2					
3		Item	Price	Amount	Total
4		Toilet rolls	1.75	4	7
5		Bread	0.85	5	4.25
6		Butter	1.65	2	3.3
7		Eggs	0.86	4	3.44
8		Teabags	2.32	3	6.96
9		Monthly Total			=E4+E5+
10					
11					

E9 ▾ *fx* =E4+E5+E6+E7+E8

A	B	C	D	E	F
Monthly Shopping Budget					
	Item	Price	Amount	Total	
	Toilet rolls	1.75	4	7	
	Bread	0.85	5	4.25	
	Butter	1.65	2	3.3	
	Eggs	0.86	4	3.44	
	Teabags	2.32	3	6.96	
	Monthly Total			24.95	

4 Once all your item prices have been multiplied by the amount of each item, you need to create a monthly total. Click in the cell under the last item in your list in column B and type 'Monthly Total'. Then, move across to column E and type '='. Click on cell E4 and type a '+'. Next, click on cell E5 and type another '+'. Continue until you have added the last item in your list and press **Return**.

5 The total of your monthly spending appears in column E. This number will be recalculated every time you change a number in your data – try altering a few numbers to see how it works. Now add another formula to subtract your monthly total from your monthly budget. Click in the cell in column B under 'Monthly Total' and type 'Monthly Budget'. Enter the value of your monthly budget in the same row in column E – in this case, '50'.

Item	Price	Amount	Total
Toilet rolls	1.75	4	7
Bread	0.85	5	4.25
Butter	1.65	2	3.3
Eggs	0.86	4	3.44
Teabags	2.32	3	6.96
Monthly Total			24.95
Monthly Budget			

Item	Price	Amount	Total
Toilet rolls	1.75	4	7
Bread	0.85	5	4.25
Butter	1.65	2	3.3
Eggs	0.86	4	3.44
Teabags	2.32	3	6.96
Monthly Total			24.95
Monthly Budget			50

Item	Price	Amount	Total
Toilet rolls	1.75	4	7
Bread	0.85	5	4.25
Butter	1.65	2	3.3
Eggs	0.86	4	3.44
Teabags	2.32	3	6.96
Monthly Total			24.95
Monthly Budget			50
Monthly Surplus			=E10-E9

Item	Price	Amount	Total
Toilet rolls	1.75	4	7
Bread	0.85	5	4.25
Butter	1.65	2	3.3
Eggs	0.86	4	3.44
Teabags	2.32	3	6.96
Monthly Total			24.95
Monthly Budget			50
Monthly Surplus			25.05
			6.2375

6 Now click under 'Monthly Budget' and type 'Monthly Surplus'. Move to column E and type an '='. Then click on your monthly budget amount, type '-', click on the monthly total amount and press **Return**. Here, the formula '=E10-E9' tells Excel to subtract the value in E9 from the value in E10. Type '=E9/4' under your surplus to divide your monthly expenditure by 4. This calculates your weekly expenditure.

Using AutoSum

Performing simple addition with Excel is easy using the formula demonstrated on the previous pages. However, if you want to add up a long list of values it can be time-consuming to enter all the cell references and plus signs into a formula. Fortunately, Excel includes an AutoSum function that instantly totals a column or row of values.

SEE ALSO...
- *Excel formulas p 24*
- *Cut, copy and paste p 32*
- *Advanced functions p 90*

BEFORE YOU START
The example below uses Excel's AutoSum function to check your bank statement and work out your expenditure. Start by opening a new spreadsheet.

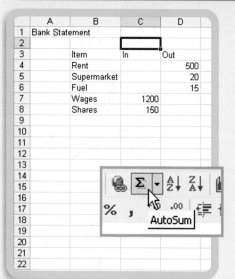

	A	B	C	D
1	Bank Statement			
2				
3		Item	In	Out
4		Rent		500
5		Supermarket		20
6		Fuel		15
7		Wages	1200	
8		Shares	150	
9				

AutoSum

1 Type a title, such as 'Bank Statement', for your spreadsheet in cell A1 and add the column headings ' Item', 'In', and 'Out'. Then copy the data from the example above. Once you have finished, select cell C2 and then click on the **AutoSum** button on the Standard toolbar.

2 When you click the **AutoSum** button, Excel inserts a **SUM function** in the selected cell. Between the brackets, Excel expects to see some information telling it which cells contain the values you want to be added together. Click and drag from cell C4 to C8 and then press **Return**.

B	C	D	E
:ment			
	=SUM(C4:C8)		
Item	In	SUM(**number1**, [number2], ...)	
Rent		500	
Supermarket		20	
Fuel		15	
Wages	1200		
Shares	150		
		5R x 1C	

C2	▼		*fx* =SUM(C4:C8)

	A	B	C	D
1	Bank Statement			
2			1350	
3		Item	In	Out
4		Rent		
5		Supermarket		
6		Fuel		
7		Wages	1200	
8		Shares	150	
9				
10				
11				
12				
13				
14				
15				

3 Excel now adds up the values in your 'In' column and displays the result in cell C2. If you select cell C2 and look in the **Formula Bar**, you will see that C2 actually contains the **AutoSum** function '=SUM(C4:C8)'. We have placed the totals above the data so you can add more entries to the bottom of the list easily without having to insert extra rows.

Watch out
When extending a range, be careful to click on the bottom corner of the blue box and not the edge, otherwise you will move the whole of the blue box down. If you accidentally move the box, use the **Undo** button to reverse your action.

	A	B	C	D
1	Bank Statement			
2			1350	
3		Item	In	Out
4		Rent		500
5		Supermarket		20
6		Fuel		15
7		Wages	1200	
8		Shares	150	
9				
10				
11			1350	535
12	Item	In	Out	
13	Rent			500
14	Supermarket			20
15	Fuel			15
16	Wages		1200	
17	Shares		150	

4 Now use the **Fill Handle** (see Copying **formulas**, page 25) to copy the **AutoSum** function into cell D2: click and drag the square at the bottom right corner of cell C2 across to D2. Excel copies the function and adds up your outgoings. The total will be displayed in cell D2 and, if you look in the **Formula Bar**, you will see the function '=SUM(D4:D8)'.

5 Next, move to cell E2 and type an '='. Click on cell C2, type a '-' and then click on cell D2. Then press **Return**. Excel will now subtract your 'Out' total from your 'In' total. The formula should read '=C2-D2'. As you add more items to your list of entries, Excel recalculates all the formulas and functions for you.

B	C	D	E
tement			
	1350	535	=C2-D2
Item	In	Out	
Rent		500	
Supermarket		20	
Fuel		15	
Wages	1200		
Shares	150		

fx =C2-D2

B	C	D	E
ement			
	1350	535	815
Item	In	Out	
Rent		500	
Supermarket		20	
Fuel		15	
Wages	1200		

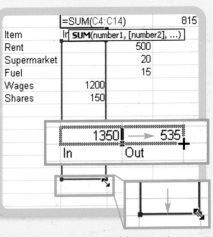

6 If you want to add some data beyond row 8 in your spreadsheet, it will not be included in the **SUM** function because we limited its range in step 1. To edit the formula, double-click on cell C2. A blue border appears around cells C4 to C8. By clicking and dragging either of the little squares at the bottom corners, it is possible to extend the formula's range ready for any new data. Copy the new formula across to cell D2 (see step 4).

Print your work

Excel's vast horizontal and vertical grid of cells means that it is usually not possible to print your data properly without first defining the area you want to print and then telling the program how to lay out the page. Fortunately, there's a Print Preview window and lots of built-in tools to assist you in fitting your data to the selected paper size.

SEE ALSO...
● *Working with page breaks p 58*
● *Viewing options p 88*

BEFORE YOU START
Excel needs to know which bits of your spreadsheet you want to print
so enter some data in a blank spreadsheet, select it, and make sure your printer is turned on.

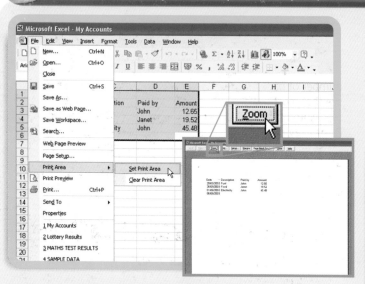

1 Click on the **File** menu, select **Print Area** and choose **Set Print Area**. Then click the **Print Preview** button. You can now see how your selected range will look when it is printed. If your data is too small, click on the **Zoom**

button to see a close-up. If there are more pages to view, either below the currently visible page or to the right of it, you will need to click the **Next** button to see them – by default, the pages are displayed down first, then across (see page 58).

2 Click on the **Setup** button. This opens the **Page Setup** dialogue box, which you can use to change the way your selected range will print. Click on the **Page** tab and first make sure

that the correct size for the paper in your printer is selected on the drop-down list next to **Paper size** – this is usually A4. If you are printing to a different paper size, select it from the list.

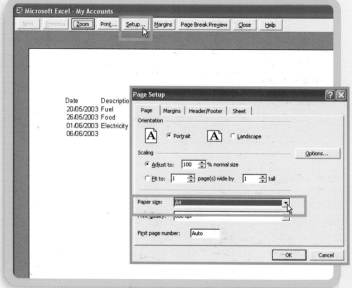

Key word
A radio button is a small circle next to an option in a dialogue box. To select the option, click once on the circle or its accompanying text, and a dot will appear. Clicking again deselects the option.

Quick printing
To print a selected area of your spreadsheet quickly, highlight the range of cells you want to print by clicking and dragging. Then click on the **File** menu and choose **Print**. Choose the 'Selection' option under 'Print what' and click the **Preview** button. Check the selection is going to print correctly and click the **Print** button.

Page Setup

Page | Margins | Header/Footer | Sheet

Orientation

A ⚪ Portrait   A 🔘 Landscape   Options...

Scaling

🔘 Adjust to: 100 % normal size
⚪ Fit to: 1 page(s) wide by 1 tall

Paper size: A4
Print quality: 600 dpi
First page number: Auto

OK   Cancel

---

3 If your data is laid out using a lot of columns, select 'Landscape' by putting a dot in the **radio button** next to this option in the **Orientation** section – this prints the page with the longest side running across so more columns can be fitted onto one page. Click on the **OK** button to return to **Print Preview** mode and see how your changes have affected the page. Click on the **Setup** button again if you want to make further changes.

4 Excel includes a useful tool that automatically fits the selected data to the width and height of a fixed number of pages. If you can see that most of your data fits the width of the page in the **Print Preview** window, click on **Setup**, select 'Fit to' under **Scaling** and select '1' next to 'page(s) wide by'. Similarly, if your data almost fits the vertical page, select '1' next to 'tall'. It may be necessary to experiment with the settings to get the right layout. For instance, your data might be printed too small if you choose one page wide for a very wide print area. To restore your data to full size, put a dot next to 'Adjust to' and enter or choose '100' in the box to the left of '% normal size'.

Page Setup

Page | Margins | Header/Footer | Sheet

Orientation

A ⚪ Portrait   A 🔘 Landscape

Scaling

⚪ Adjust to: 100 % normal size
🔘 Fit to: 1 page(s) wide by 1 tall

The Print Manager

If you change your mind after pressing the **Print** button, you can cancel the command as long as the printer hasn't started the job. A printer icon appears near the clock in the **System Tray**. Double-click on this and select the page you have just sent to the printer.

Click on the **Document** menu and select **Cancel**. Note that some printers have their own software – consult the printer manufacturer's instructions for details.

Close up
Sometimes a large spreadsheet will not fit the page correctly. When this happens, you must insert page breaks to make sure your data prints properly. For more information, see Working with page breaks, page 58.

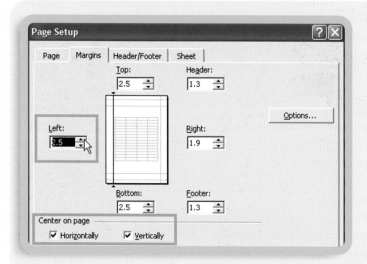

5 If you want your print area to be aligned in the middle of the page, click on the **Setup** button in the **Print Preview** window. Then select the **Margins** tab and put ticks next to 'Horizontally' and 'Vertically' under **Center on page** – a small preview pane shows how this will affect your printout. If you intend to bind your printouts to make a booklet, widen the left margin by clicking the up arrow in the **Left** box – your data will be centred between the new margins. Then click on the **OK** button to return to the **Print Preview** window.

6 Once you are happy with your print preview, click on the **Print** button. This opens the **Print** dialogue box, where you can choose a range of pages and select the number of copies to print. Click on the **OK** button when you have selected the options. You are returned to the normal view window and your page prints.

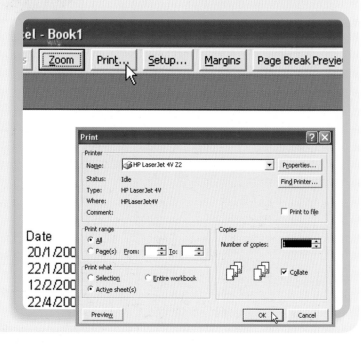

Editing Your Worksheet

Cut, copy and paste

Using Excel's Cut, Copy and Paste tools and the Office Clipboard, you can quickly move blocks of figures or text around your spreadsheet. You can also copy a formula and paste it into several cells in one go while Excel automatically changes its references. This saves time and effort if you need to move data or enter identical formulas in multiple cells.

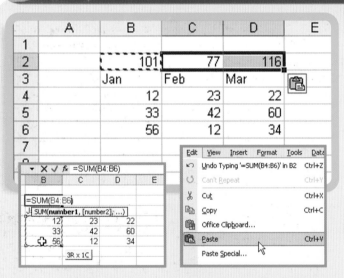

SEE ALSO...

- *Explore the program p 16*
- *Excel formulas p 24*
- *Columns and rows p 34*
- *Insert a comment p 40*

BEFORE YOU START
Enter the months 'Jan', 'Feb' and 'Mar' in cells B3, C3 and D3.

Then type in some sample figures under each column heading to use as test data.

1 Select cell B2 and insert an **AutoSum** function to total the range B4 to B6: click on the **AutoSum** button, click and drag to select cells B4 to B6 and press **Return**. The result appears in cell B2. Then click on the **Edit** menu and choose **Copy**. You will see a dotted line around cell B2. Next, select cells C2 to D2, click on the **Edit** menu and choose **Paste**. Excel pastes your function across the row and automatically adjusts it so it adds up the cells in the relevant columns.

2 To move data rather than copy it, use the **Cut** command. When you cut data, it remains in its original location on the spreadsheet until you click on **Paste** – then the original data is deleted. Try moving all your data down one row in your spreadsheet: select the range B2 to D6, click on the **Edit** menu and choose **Cut**. Then select cell B3 and click on the **Edit** menu followed by **Paste**. The data is moved to its new location. Note that copied or cut data is pasted with reference to the cell that was selected when you clicked **Paste**, in this case, B3.

Toolbar buttons

Instead of using the **Edit** menu, you can use the buttons on the Standard toolbar to cut, copy and paste. Click the downward arrow to the right of the **Paste** button to paste selectively. Or, if you prefer using the keyboard, hold down the **Ctrl** key and press **X** for cut, **C** for copy and **V** for paste.

Expert advice

You may want to paste a formula without Excel changing the range of cells to which it refers. For example, you might want to refer always to cell A1 if it contains the current VAT rate. In your formula, insert the '$' symbol before both the letter and the number so, in this case, it becomes '$A$1'. This 'fixes' the reference so that you can paste the formula anywhere and it will always refer to the specified cell for its calculations.

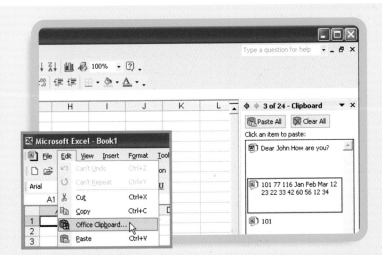

3 When you cut or copy anything in a Microsoft Office application it is placed on the **Clipboard**. You can place up to 24 items here. If you exceed 24, the oldest data will be lost. To see the **Clipboard**, click on the **Edit** menu and select **Office Clipboard**. It appears in the **Task Pane** on the right of the window. Here you can review all the items you have copied and cut – including those from other Office programs – and paste them wherever you like. Select a cell in your spreadsheet and click on the item to be pasted on the **Clipboard**. If you paste using the **Edit** menu, only the top item on the list is pasted.

4 The advantage of copying and pasting in Excel is that all the formatting and formulas are copied as well as the cell contents. However, you can choose exactly how you want your data to be pasted using the **Paste Special** feature. For example, you can choose to paste the formats only. Click on the **Edit** menu and choose **Paste Special**, then use the radio buttons and tick boxes to select how you want your data to be pasted – 'Formulas' pastes the data without any formatting, 'Values' pastes the results of formulas only, 'Comments' pastes a cell comment (see page 40), and 'Transpose' turns a column into a row or vice versa (see page 37).

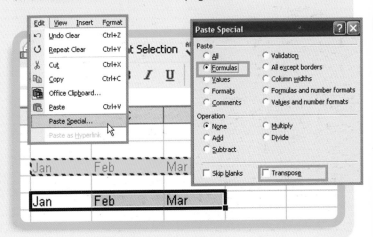

Columns and rows

Excel's grid-like structure of columns and rows makes it ideal for storing and presenting data. You can easily change the width of a column and the height of a row just by clicking and dragging. Excel also keeps track of your formulas and formatting so that inserting a row or a column doesn't change your calculations or cause problems with spreadsheet design.

SEE ALSO...
- *Format your data p 42*
- *Aligning data p 46*

BEFORE YOU START
Enter some sample text and numbers in several columns in your spreadsheet. You will need to make some text entries wider than the standard column width.

---

2 To reduce the width of the 'Amount' column, click on the boundary between columns D and E and drag it to the left until the new column width looks right. If, after changing a column width, some numbers are represented as '####', click the boundary again and widen the column slightly until all the entries fit.

1 In our example above, we have entered the column headings in Excel's default font size (10pt). However, 'Description' is too long to fit in its column. To make column C wider, move the mouse pointer over the boundary between the C and D column headers until it turns into a double-headed arrow. Then click and drag the boundary to the right – a dotted line shows your new column boundary, and a pop-up box indicates the new width in standard characters and pixels.

Expert advice
If you want to change the width of several columns in one go, select the columns by clicking on the first column header and then dragging your mouse pointer to the last header. Drag the boundary between any two of the selected column headers to widen all the columns at the same time. The same principle can be applied to rows.

Watch out
If you have entered a column of data and want to make it narrower, check that you don't cause items further down the page to overflow their cells. If you are unsure, click on the column header to select the whole column, and then click on the **Format** menu, choose **Column** and click on **AutoFit Selection**. This reduces the width to fit the largest item on the list.

	A	B	C	D
1	Home accounts			
2		Date	Description	Amount
3		20/01/2003	Fuel	£12.65
4		22/01/2003	Food	£19.00
5		12/02/2003	Electricity	£110.00
6		22/04/2003	Fuel	£5.00
7				
8				
9				
10				
11				

	A	B	C
1	Home accounts		
2		Date	Description
3		20/01/2003	Fuel
4		22/01/2003	Food
5		12/02/2003	Electricity

3 Excel automatically increases the height of rows if you increase the size of the font you are using (see page 44). However, you may want to increase the height of a row yourself to add a little space, for example, between the spreadsheet title and the column headings. Click on the boundary between the row headers, in this case rows 2 and 3, and then drag it downwards. This will increase the height of row 2 to create a little more space above the column headings. Again, a pop-up box displays the height as you drag.

4 If you want to set all the columns in a new spreadsheet to a standard width, click on the **Format** menu, choose **Column** and then select **Standard Width**. Excel's default column width is 8.43. Type in whatever value you require – in our example we have chosen 11 – and click on the **OK** button. All the columns will now be set to the selected width. Note that if you have previously adjusted the width of a column, it will not be affected by this action.

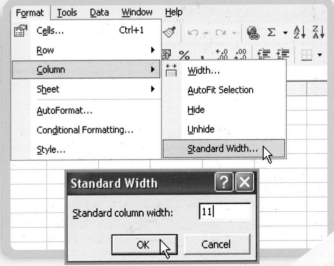

Close up
You can insert more than one column or row at a time. Click on a column or row header and drag to select the number of columns or rows you want to insert. Then click on the Insert *menu and choose* Columns *or* Rows*.*

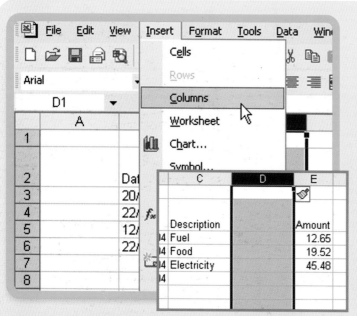

5 To insert an extra column in your spreadsheet, select the column to the right of where you want the new column by clicking on its header. For example, to insert a column between columns C and D, select column D. Then click on the **Insert** menu and choose **Columns**. The contents of D are moved to E and a new blank column is inserted after column C.

6 To insert a new row, select the row below where you want the new row, then click on the **Insert** menu and choose **Rows**. Excel moves your data down a row and inserts a new row. Don't worry about any formulas being moved, as the references are automatically changed to take into account the extra columns or rows. To remove a column or a row, select it by clicking on its header, click on the **Edit** menu and choose **Delete**. Excel moves your data and adjusts the formulas for you.

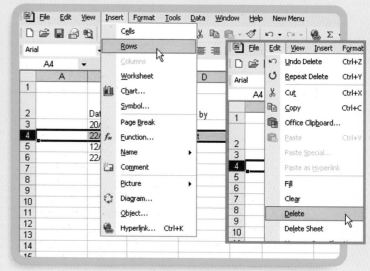

Bright idea
If you have inserted a new row and want to insert another one somewhere else, a quick way of doing this is to use the keyboard shortcut Ctrl + Y, which repeats your last action. Click on the row header below where you want the new row and use the keyboard shortcut to save time.

Watch out
If you insert several columns or rows at a time, bear in mind that Excel will only adjust the formulas if you insert rows or columns between others referred to in the formulas. For example, if an **AutoSum** function adds up the values in C2 to C5 it is best to insert a single row before C5, and use the **Ctrl + Y** keyboard shortcut to repeat the action.

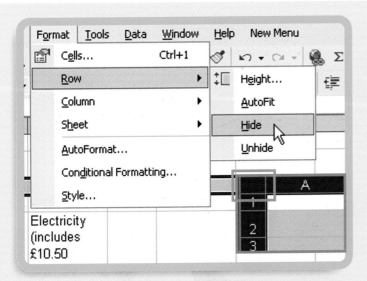

7 If you want to conceal a row but not delete it – for example, if it contains data you don't want to print or to be visible – select the row you wish to hide by clicking on the row header. Then click on the **Format** menu and select **Row** then **Hide**. To make the hidden row visible again, select the whole sheet by clicking on the **Select All** button in the top left corner, and then click on the **Format** menu and choose **Row** then **Unhide**. The same process can be applied to columns.

8 If you have typed some data in a row but then want it to be in a column, Excel has a handy transpose feature that swaps columns to rows and vice versa (see page 33). Copy the data you want to transpose by selecting it and then clicking on the **Edit** menu and selecting **Cut**. Next, select a cell on a blank area, click on the **Edit** menu and choose **Paste Special**. Put a tick next to 'Transpose' and click on the **OK** button.

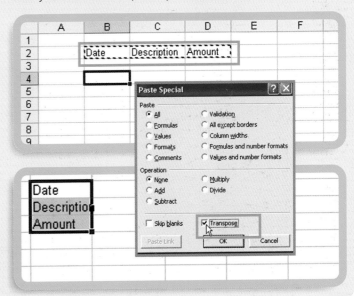

Headers and footers

You can add text or pictures to the top or bottom of every printed page using headers and footers. For example, you could add the title of your spreadsheet to the top of each page and the date of printing to the bottom right. Or, if you have a club logo, you could print it on every page. Headers and footers are only visible in the Print Preview window.

SEE ALSO...
- *Print your work* p 28
- *Style your data* p 44

BEFORE YOU START
To add a header or a footer to your spreadsheet, click on the **File** menu and choose **Page Setup**, or click the **Setup** button in **Print Preview**, and click on the **Header/Footer** tab.

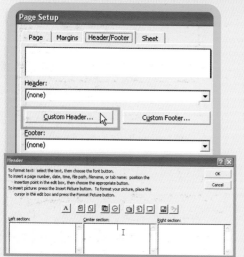

1 To insert a header, click on **Custom Header** and choose the location in which the header will appear by clicking in the corresponding white box under **Left section**, **Center section** or **Right section**. There are helpful instructions at the top of the window, to which you can refer before selecting a header.

2 Excel includes preset headers, such as date and time, for you to insert. These are available as buttons. If you do not know which button is which, click the **Help** question mark button and then click on the button in the dialogue box on which you need help. A pop-up window describes the function of the selected button. Simply select the button you want and click on **OK**.

Time buttonInserts the current time.

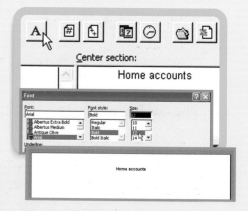

3 Alternatively, you can type your own text directly into a section. Type a title for your spreadsheet directly into your selected section. Highlight your text and click the **A** button to apply formatting (see page 44). If you want more information to appear at the top of each page, you can insert it, either in this section or in another page section, by clicking on one of the buttons or typing more text. When you have finished, click on the **OK** button twice.

Watch out

Although there is a blank space at the top and bottom of every printed page, lengthy text (or a large image) in a header or footer could 'push' your data onto additional pages when it is printed. Always check the **Print Preview** window to see the effects of your headers and footers before printing.

Bright idea

You can insert an image, for example, a company logo, in a header or footer by clicking on the Insert Picture **button under** Insert Custom Header **or** Footer. **Find the folder containing the image and click** Insert.

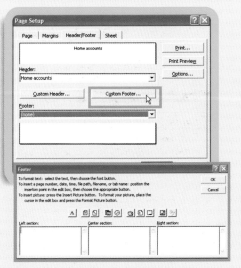

4 To add footers, click the **Custom Footer** button. You will see exactly the same range of options as in the **Custom Header** window. You can add your own text to the left, centre or right sections of the page, or choose from the range of preset options. The **Left section** box is automatically selected.

5 Click the **File Name** button with a tiny open folder icon. This inserts the code '&[Path]&[File]' in the **Left section** box, which tells Excel to print the file name of your spreadsheet at the bottom left of every page. The '[Path]' section of the code tells Excel to print the folders as well as the file name. This is useful for tracking down the file on your PC.

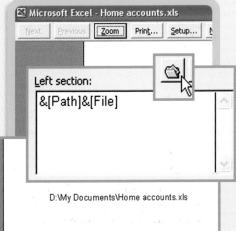

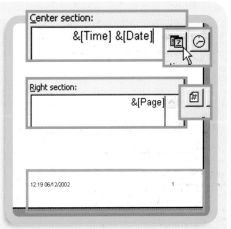

6 Select the **Center section** box and click the **Time** button. Then press the **Spacebar** once and click the **Date** button. This tells Excel to print the time and the date on which the spreadsheet was printed, which is useful for tracking multiple printouts of the same document. Finally, click in the **Right section** box and click the **Page Number** button followed by **OK** twice. Click the **Print Preview** button to check your headers and footers on the page.

Insert a comment

A spreadsheet may contain data or formulas that the user may not understand, but it is not always convenient to type notes directly on to the sheet. However, you can add pop-up comments to any cell. Each cell with an attached comment has a small red triangle in the top-right corner – the comment only appears while the mouse pointer is hovering over the cell.

SEE ALSO...
- *Explore the program p 16*
- *Cut, copy and paste p 32*

WORKING WITH COMMENTS

Open a file you have created already, or set up a new one containing some sample data.

Add a comment

To insert a comment, first select the cell to which you want to attach the comment, then click on the **Insert** menu and choose **Comment**. A small window pops up, into which you can enter some explanatory text. Click away from the comment when you have finished typing. A red triangle is displayed in the top right of the cell indicating there is a comment attached.

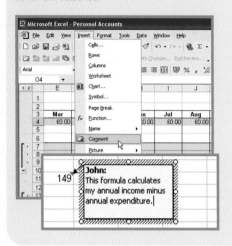

Read a comment

Now, move the mouse pointer over the cell. The comment pops up and remains visible while the pointer is over the cell. To edit the comment, first select the cell, then click on the **Insert** menu and choose **Edit comment**. To remove a comment, select the cell, click on the **Edit** menu and choose **Clear** followed by **Comments**. As a shortcut, you can right-click the cell and choose **Edit Comment** or **Delete Comment** from the pop-up menu.

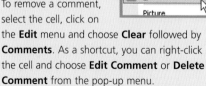

Viewing all comments

If you want to see all the comments on your spreadsheet, click on the **View** menu and choose **Comments**. All your comments will be displayed next to their cells. You can click and drag them around by their edges if one comment is obscuring another.

Printing comments

You can print comments, either as they appear on the spreadsheet when you view them, or at the bottom of the last printed page. Click on the **File** menu and choose **Page Setup**. Then click on the **Sheet** tab and choose 'As displayed on sheet' in the **Comments** box to print your comments where they appear, or 'At end of sheet' if you don't want your data to be obscured by the comment boxes.

Reviewing comments

The **Reviewing** toolbar has a range of options that enable you to make quick changes to your comments. Click on the **View** menu, choose **Toolbars** then **Reviewing**. The first button enables you to edit the comment and the right and left arrow buttons move you through the spreadsheet one comment at a time. The next buttons show and hide comments, and the button with the cross deletes a comment.

Formatting Your Worksheet

Format your data

Excel needs to know the type of data stored in each of its cells in order to display, sort and calculate it correctly. When you enter certain information – such as dates – Excel will often apply the correct formatting automatically. However, there is a surefire way to make sure Excel formats all your categories of data correctly, no matter how you type them in.

SEE ALSO...
- *Columns and rows* p 34
- *Style your data* p 44
- *Aligning data* p 46

BEFORE YOU START
Type the headings 'Date', 'Description' and 'Amount' in cells B2 to D2. This example shows you how to format cells to display data as dates and currency.

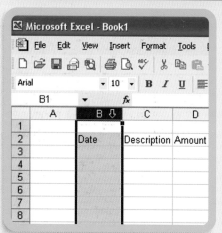

1 Once you have typed the headings for the columns of data in your spreadsheet, it's a good idea to format the cells before you start entering the data. That way, Excel will automatically insert the '£' sign in the prices, and will also differentiate between text and dates. Highlight the column of cells which will contain your dates by clicking on the column header – in this case B.

2 Click on the **Format** menu and choose **Cells**. When the **Format Cells** dialogue box opens, click on the **Number** tab and choose **Date** from the **Category** list on the left. You will see a selection of date formats appear in the 'Type' list on the right. Scroll down until you see a format you like and click on it. Use a short version (shown below) for large spreadsheets.

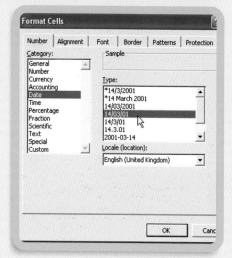

3 Click on the **OK** button to apply the formatting to the selected cells. Now try entering the date in cell B3 as '20 Jan 2003'. Excel recognises you have typed in a date and formats it as '20/01/03', the format we selected in step 2. Any date typed in column B will be formatted this way.

Watch out
If your date column appears to be full of strange numbers, you may have formatted it incorrectly. Don't change any data, just select the date range, click on the **Format** menu and choose **Cells**. Then click the **Number** tab and make sure that 'Date' is selected in the list on the left.

Expert advice
Try out the other formatting options under the **Number** tab in the **Format Cells** dialogue box. You can instruct Excel to round numbers to two decimal points, format your numbers as times with AM and PM, or even display figures as fractions or percentages.

5 Click on D at the top of the 'Amount' column to select the whole column, then open the **Format Cells** dialogue box again and, under the **Number** tab, choose 'Currency' from the **Category** list. Select a **£** sign from the list under **Symbol** and then choose how you would like negative numbers to be displayed – select the first option. Click on **OK**.

4 Next, select the 'Description' column by clicking on the C column header. Then click on the **Format** menu and choose **Cells**. Since the **Number** tab is still selected, click on 'Text' in the list on the left and click on **OK**. This ensures that everything entered in the 'Description' column, even if it looks like a number, will be treated and sorted as text.

6 Now start entering data into your spreadsheet – type dates in the first column, text entries in the second and amounts in the third. You will see that Excel automatically formats each new entry according to the pre-selected cell formatting. Note that text is aligned to the left of each cell and numbers to the right. It is easy to change the alignment settings – see page 46 for details.

Style your data

No matter how well your spreadsheet calculates its data, the results are wasted if its contents are not clearly presented and legible. Excel includes a wide range of data formatting tools, including options for sizing, styling and colouring data, which enable you to turn a bewildering array of figures and calculations into an easy-to-follow and logical worksheet.

SEE ALSO...
- *Format your data p 42*
- *Colours and patterns p 48*

BEFORE YOU START
Enter some sample data into your spreadsheet and select the cells by clicking and dragging the mouse from the first cell to the last cell in your desired range.

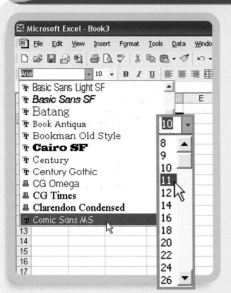

1 To change font type and size, use the **Font** and **Font Size** boxes on the **Formatting** toolbar. Click the small downward arrow to the right of each box to choose from a list of options. If you want to format some data within a specific cell, highlight only the words or figures you want to format.

2 You can use the **Bold**, **Italic** and **Underline** font style buttons to quickly style selected data. However, bear in mind that both italic and underline can be difficult to read on a large page of relatively small data.

Date	Description	Amount
20/1/2004	Fuel	12.65
22/1/2004	Food	19.52
12/2/2004	Electricity	45.48

Date	Description	Amount
20/1/2004	Fuel	12.65
22/1/2004	Food	19.52
12/2/2004	Electricity	45.48

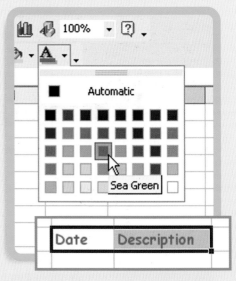

3 You can colour selected data by clicking the down arrow beside the **A** button on the far right of the **Formatting** toolbar and choosing a colour from the pop-up palette. Note that if you click the **A** button instead of the arrow, your data will change to the colour of the bar underneath the **A**, which indicates the last colour selected.

Choosing a font

Excel uses the Arial font by default. This means that all data will be Arial and is sized at 10pt until you change the style. Arial is a sans-serif font, which means it has no 'tails' on the ends of the strokes of each character. It is used in Excel because it is better suited to numbers and is more legible at larger font sizes. Serif

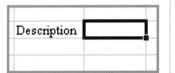

fonts, such as Times New Roman (shown above), are more suitable for use in long segments of small sized text and are used typically in word processor documents.

Watch out
If you combine too many fonts and colours on one spreadsheet it can become illegible and confusing. Stick to one or two fonts of no more than two sizes, make sure that your use of colours does not make the data illegible when it's printed, and use bold formatting judiciously.

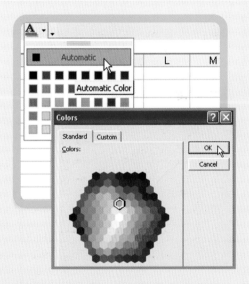

5 If you want to make several changes – font size, style and colour – to a selected range of cells all in one go, you can do this using the **Format Cells** dialogue box. Click on the **Format** menu and choose **Cells**. The **Font** tab gives you control over all the style options on the **Formatting** toolbar plus an extended range of font effects. The **Preview** pane displays how your changes will affect the selected cells once you click on **OK**.

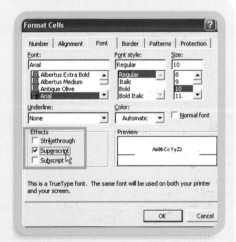

4 To revert to black data, choose **Automatic Color** from the **Font Color** palette. If a colour you want is not on the palette, click on the **Tools** menu, choose **Options** and select the **Color** tab. Pick a colour you want to change and click on the **Modify** button. Then select a new colour from the hexagonal palette and click **OK** twice.

6 There are a few advanced data-formatting options available in the **Effects** section under the **Font** tab. Strikethrough can be used to indicate data that is redundant but that you do not want to delete, for example, '~~Overdue~~'. Superscript positions text, such as 'th' or 'rd', above the line – as in '4th' and '3rd'. Subscript is used for text you want to position below the line, such as the '2' in 'H_2O'.

Aligning data

By default, Excel positions numbers to the right of cells and text to the left. However, you can position your data any way you like – for instance, the heading above a column of figures looks much better if it is aligned to the right. Excel has a number of alignment options that you can use to style your spreadsheet and make your data more comprehensible.

SEE ALSO...
- *Columns and rows p 34*
- *Format your data p 42*

BEFORE YOU START
Create a spreadsheet similar to the one used in the Style your data project (page 44). Note how Excel aligns the text to the left and the numbers to the right of a cell.

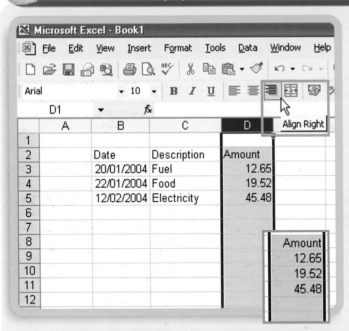

1 You can use the **Left**, **Center** and **Right align** buttons on the **Formatting** toolbar to quickly align text in a selected range of cells. Click on the header of a column that contains both numbers and text, and click on the **Align Right** button. Repeat for any other columns that contain a mixture of text and figures.

2 Click on the **Format** menu, then on **Cells** and select the **Alignment** tab to see more alignment options. You can choose to indent text or control the vertical alignment of data in rows (see Vertical alignment box, above right) and, under **Orientation**, there is an option to display your data at an angle.

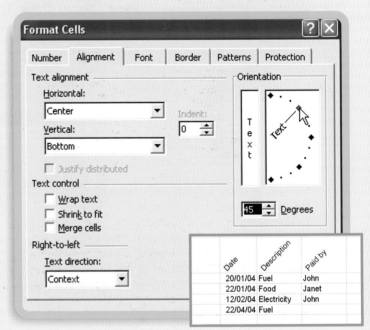

Vertical alignment

If you use the Wrap text option – see Step 3 – you should align the data to the top of the cells. This makes it easier to read the row. Highlight all the rows that will contain the wrapped data, excluding any column headings. Open the **Format Cells** dialogue box and, under the **Alignment** tab, choose 'Top' from the **Vertical** list box.

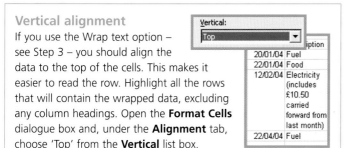

Watch out
Although text can be centred or aligned anywhere in a cell, numbers should always be aligned to the right, otherwise they become difficult to read. This is because the numbers will not line up correctly in a column of figures.

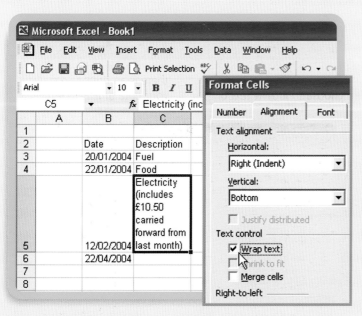

3 If you have entered more data into a cell than will fit across its width, select the cell and open the **Format Cells** dialogue box again. Then click on the **Alignment** tab and put a tick next to 'Wrap text' under **Text control**. This forces Excel to expand the cell downwards so that all your data is visible – see page 34 for information on changing column widths and row heights.

4 You can also merge two cells to create a single cell the size of the two original cells. Just select two or more cells and tick the 'Merge cells' option. In the example below, the cells above 'IN' and 'OUT' have been merged to provide enough space for the headings, which were then centred. You can also use the **Merge and Center** button on the **Formatting** toolbar as a shortcut to merge cells. This will automatically apply the center alignment to the merged cells.

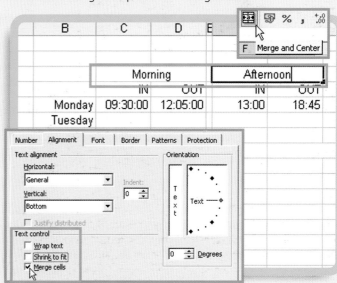

Colours and patterns

Excel includes a range of useful tools to add shades and patterns to cells. Colouring sections of a spreadsheet draws the reader's attention to important figures, and makes it easier to enter and read data in multiple columns. When used in conjunction with Excel's data styling features, these tools can enhance your work, both on screen and on the printed page.

SEE ALSO...
- *Using AutoSum* p 26
- *Style your data* p 44

BEFORE YOU START
Set up a spreadsheet with some sample dates, text and amounts in columns with headings. Add up the amounts using the **AutoSum** function (see page 26).

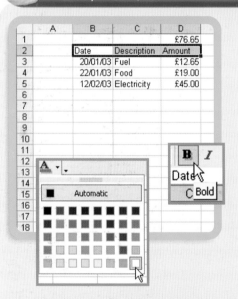

1 First, click and drag to select the cells that contain the column headings 'Date', 'Description' and 'Amount'. Then click on the downward arrow next to the **Font Color** button and make the text white. Finally, click on the **Bold** button to embolden the text.

2 To the left of the **Font Color** button is the **Fill Color** button – it has a bucket icon on it. With the row of data you just formatted still highlighted, click the small downward arrow next to the **Fill Color** button and choose the **Black** square from the palette. This colours the background of the selected cells black.

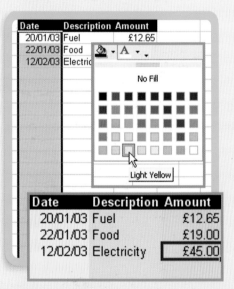

3 Select 50 rows of the 'Date' column (excluding the heading) by clicking and dragging down, and use the **Fill Color** palette to choose the **Light Yellow** colour. Leave the font colour as black. Choose different pale colour backgrounds for the 'Description' and 'Amount' columns in the same way.

Watch out
Be careful that the cell colour does not clash with the font colour. If you choose a dark fill, make the data a light colour so it stands out. If you are printing in black and white, coloured data will print as black, and won't show up against a dark fill, so choose white data.

Expert advice
If you normally print to a colour printer, but want a black and white printout of a coloured spreadsheet, there's no need to reformat all the cells to make the data visible. Click on the **File** menu and choose **Page Setup**. Then click the **Sheet** tab and put a tick next to 'Black and white'.

B	C	D
		£655.18
Date	**Description**	**Amount**
20/01/03	Fuel	£12.65
22/01/03	Food	£19.00
12/02/03	Electricity	£45.00
14/02/03	Food	£85.00
01/03/03	Food	£64.15
05/04/03	Food	£27.50
19/04/03	Fuel	£25.50
22/04/03	Fuel	£5.00
05/05/03	Insurance	£250.00
16/05/03	Electricity	£29.63
23/05/03	MOT	£55.00
23/05/03	Food	£36.75
24/05/03	Fuel	

4 Click on the cell containing the **AutoSum** formula. Use the **Fill Color** button to make it bright yellow. Now the 'Total' is clearly visible and the eye can easily scan down the columns of data, making it easier to enter and read information.

5 If you want to apply a background pattern and a colour to a cell, you can use the **Format Cells** dialogue box. One advantage of this method is that you can see a preview of how the cell will look before clicking the **OK** button. Click on the **Format** menu and choose **Cell**, then click the **Patterns** tab. Use the palettes to select a colour and the drop-down list next to **Pattern** to choose a background pattern. Check the results under **Sample** and when you are happy, click on the **OK** button.

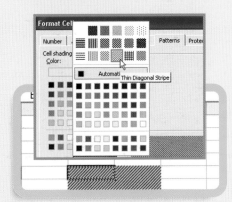

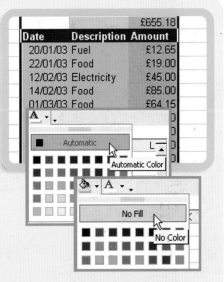

6 To quickly remove fill and font colours from your spreadsheet, select the range of cells, as above, click on the **Font Color** button and choose **Automatic** from the top of the palette. Then click the **Fill Color** button and choose **No Fill**. This makes your text black and removes the fill colour from your cells.

Borders

On screen, Excel's grid is divided up by vertical and horizontal gridlines that act as guides for cell selection and data entry, and which, under normal circumstances, do not appear on the printed page. However, you can add borders to underscore and divide areas of your spreadsheet to increase its visual impact and make it easier to use.

SEE ALSO...
- *Style your data* p 44
- *Colours and patterns* p 48

BEFORE YOU START
There are three ways to add borders – via a button, a special toolbar or the **Format Cells** dialogue box. First, open a new spreadsheet and insert some data.

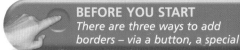

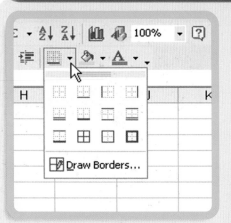

1 You can use the **Borders** button on the **Formatting** toolbar to choose from a selection of borders. This button is positioned to the left of the **Fill Color** button and displays either a grid of dots with a black line underneath, or the last type of border you used. Select all the cells around which you want to add a border and click the downward arrow on the right of the button to open a palette of 12 preset borders.

2 Each of the preset options only affects the border shown on the button. This means you can add a bottom border by clicking the grid with the black line at the bottom, and then add a left border to the same cells by using the left border button. The borders will surround the selected range of cells as a whole, unless you use the **All Borders** button, which puts a border around each selected cell in the range.

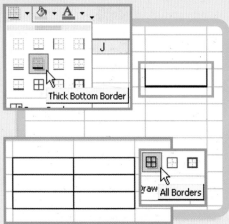

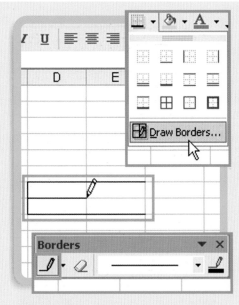

3 If you prefer, you can draw the borders directly onto your sheet. Click on the **Borders** button and choose **Draw Borders**. A toolbar pops up. Use the pencil on the left to click on the lines to which you want to add a border – use the **Undo** button on the Standard toolbar if you make an error.

Watch out
Avoid applying the same border to every cell. This will create a dark grid, which can make it difficult for the reader's eye to follow the columns and rows. If you want to print a grid, apply heavier lines to vertical gridlines and choose a dotted line for horizontal gridlines.

Copying cell formats
If you have formatted a cell or range of cells with a background colour, data style and borders, you can copy the formatting to another cell or range of cells. Select the formatted cells and click on the **Format Painter** button. Then, select the cells you want to change. The selected cells take the formatting of the original ones.

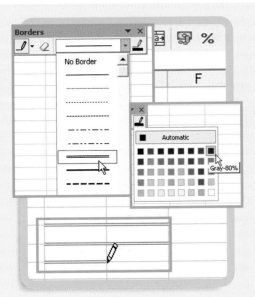

4 By default, a thin black border is selected. However, you can use the drop-down lists to choose a different line type and border colour. Click on the downward arrow to the right of the horizontal line to choose a new line type and then click on the right pencil button to choose a colour.

5 If you want to add a mixture of border styles to a range of cells – for instance, if you want all cells in the range to have vertical thin black sides and dotted grey tops – use the **Format Cells** dialogue box. Highlight a range of cells, click on the **Format** menu and select **Cells** to open the **Format Cells** box. Then click on the **Border** tab. Select a border from the range under **Style** in the **Line** section.

6 Use the grid under **Border** to position each border: either click where you want each border to go or use the **Outline** and **Inside** buttons under **Presets**. If you want to change a border, select a new style and click on the unwanted border to replace it. Click on the border again to remove it completely. Use the **None** button under **Presets** to remove all the borders.

Automatic formatting

If you have entered column and row headings and some data into a range of cells, Excel's AutoFormat feature enables you to select font and cell colours and borders from a range of built-in styles, and apply them with a single click. You can even specify which elements of a style to apply and see a preview of the results before you click on the OK button.

SEE ALSO...
- *Style your data* p 44
- *Colours and patterns* p 48
- *Borders* p 50

BEFORE YOU START
Type 'Maths Test Results' in cell A1 and format this as bold and 14pt.

Then enter month headings down column A, starting in cell A4. Enter names across row 3 from cell B3.

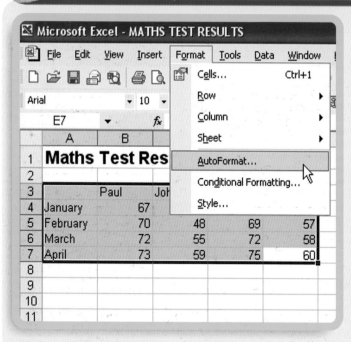

1 Highlight all the data and headings in your sample spreadsheet by clicking and dragging from the top left cell across and down to the bottom right cell. The selected area will turn light blue. Click on the **Format** menu and choose **AutoFormat**.

2 When the **AutoFormat** box opens, scroll down the styles until you find one you like and click once on it. Then click **OK** to see how the style looks when applied to your data. If you don't like the results, click on the **Undo** button on the **Standard** toolbar and try again.

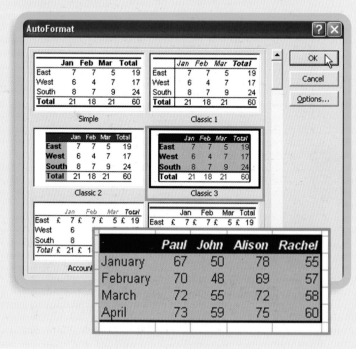

Expert advice
Once you've applied an **AutoFormat**, you can still alter the formats yourself using the **Font Color**, **Fill Color** and **Borders** tools.

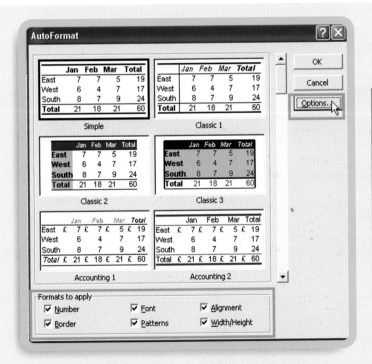

3 If you want to apply certain elements of the preset style to your data, but not others, click the **Options** button in the **AutoFormat** box. Two rows of tick boxes will appear at the bottom of the window.

4 Choose a style from the list and remove the ticks next to those elements you do not want to be styled automatically. You'll see your changes reflected in the preview windows. Finally, click on the **OK** button.

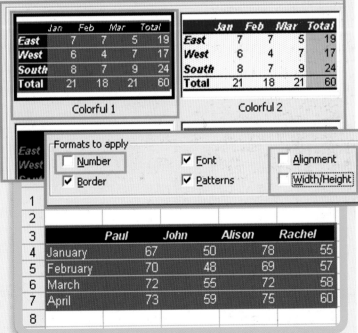

Style and format options

Formatting cells and values in a large spreadsheet can be time-consuming, but you can speed up the process by using the Style tool, which allows you to apply a range of styles in one go. Conditional Formatting is another useful feature, which searches your spreadsheet for values that meet certain conditions, then formats those cells to make them stand out.

SEE ALSO...
- *Format your data* p 42
- *Style your data* p 44

SAVING STYLES

You may have applied font, cell colour and border styles to ranges in your spreadsheet. If you want to re-apply these quickly in other spreadsheets, you can create a handy list of styles.

Click on the **Format** menu and then select **Style**. Type a short recognisable name for your new style next to **Style name** and remove the ticks next to the options you don't want to use in your style. Then click on the **Modify** button. This opens the **Format Cells** dialogue box.

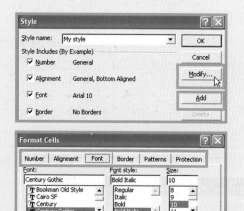

Use the tabs to select the formats for your style, and then click on **OK**. Then click the **Add** button in the **Style** dialogue box to put your new style on the list. You can add as many styles as you like in this way. Click **OK** and **OK**

again to return to the spreadsheet. To apply the new styles, select the range of cells to which you want to apply the formatting, click on the **Format** menu and choose **Style**. Then select your style from the list and click the **OK** button.

Test Results			
Paul	John	Alison	Rachel
67	50	78	55
70	48	69	57
72	55	72	58

Bright idea
To remove all styles from a range of cells, highlight the range, click on the Format *menu and choose* Style*. Then choose 'Normal' from the list next to* Style name *and click* OK.

Expert advice
If you have created some named styles in a spreadsheet and want to use them elsewhere, open the spreadsheet in which the styles are saved, then open the new sheet. Click on the **Format** menu and choose **Style**. Click the **Merge** button and, under **Merge styles from**, select the name of your first spreadsheet. When you click on **OK**, all the new styles will be available for you to use.

CONDITIONAL FORMATTING

Excel can highlight cells that contain data matching certain criteria. One useful way of using this feature is to make Excel change the font colour of all test scores over 70, say, to blue on a yellow background, in order to draw the reader's attention to those items.

Select the cells in the table, excluding the column and row headings, then click on the **Format** menu and choose **Conditional Formatting**. Under **Condition 1**, make sure that 'Cell Value Is' is selected from the drop-down list. In the next drop-down list, choose 'greater than' and type '70' in the box on the right. Click the **Format** button and select the **Font** tab. Under **Color**, select blue from the drop-down list. Choose 'Bold' from the list under **Font Style**. Then click the **Patterns** tab and choose a yellow colour. Click **OK** and then **OK** again to return to your spreadsheet.

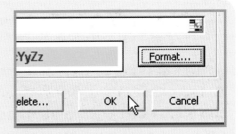

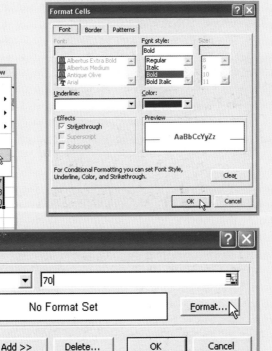

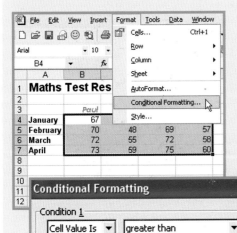

Any values in the scores table that exceed 70 will be highlighted. If you don't have any scores this large, temporarily change one of the scores to test the formatting.

	A	B	C	D	E
1	**Maths Test Results**				
2					
3		Paul	John	Alison	Rachel
4	January	67	50	78	55
5	February	70	48	69	57
6	March	72	55	72	58
7	April	73	59	75	60
8					

You can apply font colour, borders and cell colours for up to three sets of **conditions**. For example, add a second condition that locates scores under 50 and turns them green.

	A	B	C	D	E
1	**Maths Test Results**				
2					
3		Paul	John	Alison	Rachel
4	January	67	50	78	55
5	February	70	48	69	57
6	March	72	55	72	58
7	April	73	59	75	60
8					

Key word
*Conditions **are stipulations that must be fulfilled before an action is performed, for example '=0'. In this case, if the data in the cell is zero, then the cell will be highlighted with the chosen formatting.***

Removing conditional formatting
Conditional formatting works on the cells selected when you first applied the format. To remove it, you must select the cells from which you want to remove the formatting, click on the **Format** menu and choose **Conditional Formatting** followed by **Delete**. Then tick the conditions you want to remove and click on **OK** and **OK** again.

Templates and solutions

Excel has several built-in templates called 'Spreadsheet Solutions'. These are spreadsheets that have been designed and formatted in advance, ready for you to type in your own data. More spreadsheet templates are available from the Microsoft Web site. All these templates and solutions can be accessed via the New Workbook panel on the Task Pane.

SEE ALSO...
● *Format your data* p 42

BEFORE YOU START
*Click on the **View** menu and choose **Task Pane**. If the New Workbook panel is not visible, click the down arrow at the top and choose 'New Workbook'.*

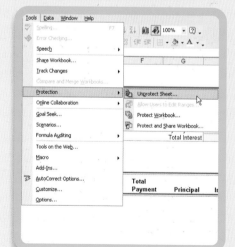

1 The templates are listed on the **Task Pane** under **New from template**. To try out a useful loan calculator spreadsheet that is supplied with Excel, click on **General Templates** and choose the **Spreadsheet Solutions** tab. Click on **Loan Amortization** and then click on the **OK** button.

2 Because the spreadsheet was designed in the USA, it will display the amounts and results of its calculations in dollars. However, the formulas still work correctly. If you want to convert the currency format to use the '£' symbol, click on the **Tools** menu, choose **Protection** and select **Unprotect Sheet**. This allows you to edit all the cells in the spreadsheet.

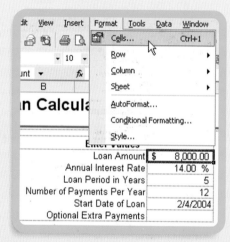

3 Now enter some values into the sheet. Type '8000' into cell D6 to the right of 'Loan Amount', then '14' as the annual interest rate, '5' as the loan period and '12' as the payments per year. Enter the current date next to 'Start Date of Loan' and press **Return**. To change the '$' symbols to '£' symbols, select the first cell that contains a number preceded by a '$' symbol, click on the **Format** menu and choose **Cells**.

Watch out

Microsoft Office was designed in the USA so some of its built-in templates may be formatted in a way that is inappropriate for the United Kingdom. Look out for 'Zip' instead of 'Postcode' and 'State' instead of 'County'. You can edit these by unprotecting the worksheet (see step 2).

Quick repeat

If you apply the '£' currency formatting to a range of cells using the **Format Cells** dialogue box, you don't need to use the box to repeat the process. Simply select the next cell or range of cells, hold down the **Ctrl** key on the keyboard and press **Y**. This keyboard shortcut repeats your last action. You can use it as many times as you like.

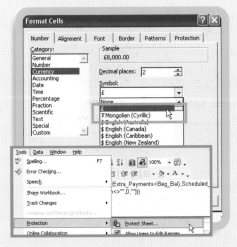

4 Click the **Number** tab and select 'Currency' from the list on the left. Under **Symbol** on the right, choose '£' from the drop-down list and click **OK**. Repeat this process for all the individual cells and ranges on the sheet that contain a '$' symbol. Once you've finished, click on the **Tools** menu, choose **Protection** and select **Protect Sheet**. Click **OK** and save your loan calculator with a different name.

5 Now you can use the spreadsheet to compare loans from different providers, and to try out a range of payment options on each loan. Type each set of data in the cells at the top as before. The grid of cells from row 18 down displays the amount per month, the due date, what proportion is interest and how much is outstanding at a given date. Print or save each version as a new name.

Pmt No.	Payment Date	Beginning Balance	Scheduled Payment
1	07/02/2004	£8,000.00	£186.15
2	07/03/2004	7,907.19	186.15
3	07/04/2004	7,813.29	186.15
4	07/05/2004	7,718.30	186.15
5	07/06/2004	7,622.20	186.15
6	07/07/2004	7,524.98	186.15
7	07/08/2004	7,426.63	186.15
8	07/09/2004	7,327.12	186.15
9	07/10/2004	7,226.46	186.15
10	07/11/2004	7,124.62	186.15
11	07/12/2004	7,021.60	186.15
12	07/01/2005	6,917.37	186.15
13	07/02/2005	6,811.93	186.15
14	07/03/2005	6,705.26	186.15
15	07/04/2005	6,597.34	186.15
16	07/05/2005	6,488.16	186.15

Amortization Table

6 There are additional templates, both for Excel and for other Office applications, on Microsoft's Web site. You can find these by clicking on **Templates on Microsoft.com** on the **Task Pane**. This launches your Web browser and, if you are connected to the Internet, opens the Office Templates Web page. Here you'll find lots of templates for all the Office programs, arranged under category headings.

Working with page breaks

If you print a large spreadsheet, Excel will automatically split the data into sections according to the size of the paper in your printer. As a result, linked information may be divided over two pages, or headings may be split from related data. But, by using page breaks, you can instruct Excel to print your data the way you want it to be seen.

SEE ALSO...
- *Print your work p 28*
- *Columns and rows p 34*
- *Headers and footers p 38*

BEFORE YOU START
Open your loan calculator spreadsheet (page 56). Click on the File *menu, choose* **Page Setup** *and make sure 'A4 paper' is selected and the* **Scaling** *is set to 100%.*

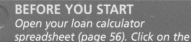

1 Click on the **View** menu and choose **Page Break Preview**. Click on **OK** if you see a **Welcome to Page Break Preview** window. Excel's automatic page breaks are marked by blue dotted lines. Scroll down the page and see how the pages will be printed – first down your sheet, then across one column and down again. Page numbers are superimposed on the worksheet in grey letters. You can change this page order in the **Page Setup** dialogue box to 'Over, then down'.

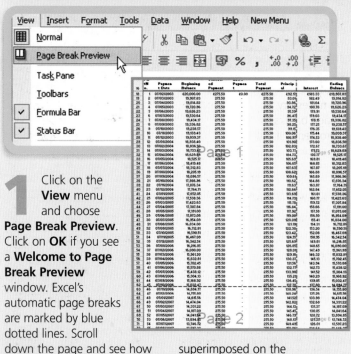

2 In this example, two columns of data – 'Interest' and 'Ending Balance' – are overflowing onto pages five and six. Click the vertical blue dotted line and drag it to the right to include all your columns.

You can move the horizontal breaks too. This drag and drop method of moving page breaks works well for spreadsheets with only two or three pages but for larger spreadsheets you should insert manual page breaks.

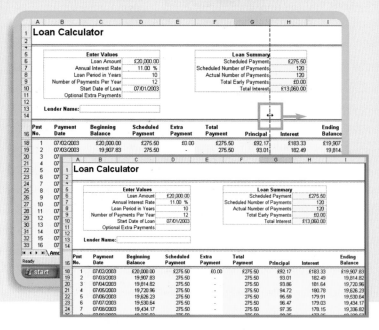

Using Graphics

Drawing in Excel

Excel is equipped with graphical tools that you can use to enhance your spreadsheets. You can insert an illustration or photograph, place transparent arrows on your sheet to bring attention to important items, and even draw freehand on top of the data. The Drawing toolbar offers easy access to these and many other useful graphical options.

SEE ALSO...
- *Style your data* p 44
- *Colours and patterns* p 48

Drawing tools

Excel's most-used graphics tools are placed on the **Drawing** toolbar as buttons – these include the line tool as well as tools for drawing arrows, rectangles and ovals. Hold the **Shift** key down while drawing to create a square or circle.

Text box

A **Text Box** is a free-floating rectangle into which you can type text. You can position it anywhere on your spreadsheet, perhaps as a printable note to users (if you want to add a non-printing note, see Insert a comment, page 40). Click the **Text Box** button then click and drag on your spreadsheet to create the box. Click on the edges to select the box and within it to type in some text. Click and drag a corner to resize the box and an edge to reposition it.

£100.00	£100.00	£100.00	£100.00
£20.75	£45.00	£4.50	£6.00
£526.17	£547.41	£501.25	£501.91

Remember - include insurance costs, due at the end of the year.

WordArt

The WordArt tool enables you to add free-floating text effects to your spreadsheet. Click the button, choose from a range of styles and click **OK**. Then type your text and choose a font, size and format (bold or italic) and click **OK** again. The stylised text appears in the window. Click and drag the corners to move or resize it. The **WordArt** toolbar enables you to edit the content, shape and style of the text.

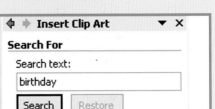

Birthdays

Clip Art

The Insert **Clip Art** feature displays a huge searchable range of stylised cartoons and photographs that you can position in your spreadsheet for fun or to add visual interest. You'll need the 'Microsoft Office XP Media Content' disk if you want to use **Clip Art**. Click on the **Insert Clip Art** button to open the **Clip Art Task Pane**. Type a word that represents the type of picture you are looking for under **Search text**. Under **Results should be**, choose to

search 'Clip Art', 'Photographs', 'Movies' or 'Sounds' by ticking the appropriate boxes. Then click on **Search**. Excel returns thumbnail images of all items matching your keyword.

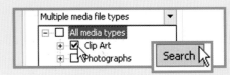

Scroll down the list until you see an image that you want to insert into your spreadsheet, then click on it. You can resize it using the corner and side handles, or move it by clicking and dragging. In the example below, the image has been moved behind the WordArt by clicking on the **Draw** menu and choosing **Order** then **Send to back**.

Insert a picture

You may want to place a picture in an Excel spreadsheet. It could be a company or club logo, or just reference material for a list of objects. Use the **Insert Picture** button to browse to the folder on your hard disk where your logo or picture is stored. Click on the image you want to insert and then click the **Insert** button.

Fill, line and font colours

The next three buttons on the **Drawing** toolbar are the **Fill Color** (see page 48 for more details), **Line Color** and **Font Color** (see page 44) tools. The **Line Color** button enables you to change the colour of a selected line.

Line style

You can also choose the thickness of a line using the **Line Style** button, and whether it is dotted or dashed using the **Dash Style** button. Any line can be turned into an arrow with the **Arrow Style** button. Click on **More Arrows** to see more options.

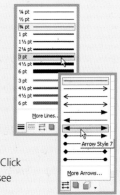

Shadow Style and 3-D

Many of the **AutoShapes** can be given a shadow or can have a 3-D effect applied by clicking on the **Shadow Style** and **3-D Style** buttons. Experiment with the tools to see which style suits your spreadsheet. Click the **Settings** buttons to see a toolbar with extra options. Use the **No Shadow** and **No 3-D** buttons at the top of the pop-up menus to remove any formatting.

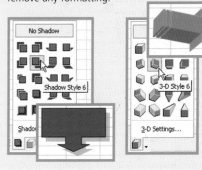

Fill effects

Click the **Fill Color** button and choose **Fill effects**. Under the **Gradient** tab you can select a fill that starts with one colour and ends with another. Under **Texture** there are some built-in wood, stone and material fills – just select one and click **OK** to apply it. The **Pattern** tab allows you to apply stripes and dots and the **Picture** tab enables you to fill a selected area with a picture.

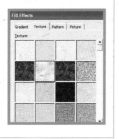

Add a chart

If your spreadsheet contains a series of numbers that change over time, showing a trend or a pattern, a chart can give you an instant overview. You can see at a glance whether your spending is increasing, or easily compare one set of figures with another. Excel's Chart Wizard gives step-by-step guidance and offers a range of colourful 2-D and 3-D charts.

SEE ALSO...
● *Colours and patterns* p 48

BEFORE YOU START
Presenting your household finances in the form of a barchart *makes it easier to analyse the data. Open your Family Budget Planner spreadsheet (see page 60).*

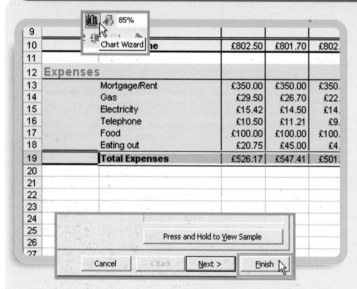

1 In order for Excel to create a chart, you must first select the data you want to be included. Select the cells from row 19 containing your total expenses, including the heading but excluding the last 'Total' cell. Click on the **Chart Wizard** button on the **Standard** toolbar then click on the **Finish** button. Excel will insert a simple barchart on top of your data showing how your expenses vary from month to month.

2 You can move the chart by clicking anywhere on the white area around it (but not on your spreadsheet) and dragging it across your spreadsheet – the cursor changes to a cross and a dotted outline shows the new position. Resize a chart by clicking on a corner box and dragging to a new size. Note that the **Chart** toolbar pops up whenever a chart is selected. This provides a number of options for modifying the appearance and format of your chart.

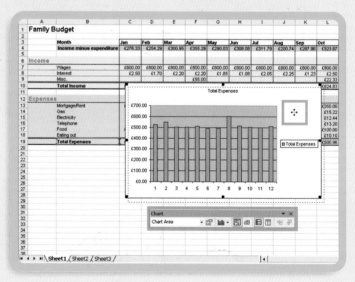

Close up
You can edit your chart to suit your needs. To change the colour of any section of a chart, just double-click on the part you want to modify and select a new colour. If the numbers on the Y axis are too large, double-click on them and choose a smaller font size.

Expert advice
If the **Chart** toolbar is not visible when you click on your new chart, click on the **View** menu, then on **Toolbars** and put a tick next to 'Chart'.

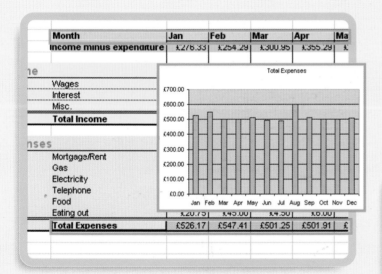

4 To create a chart that displays the difference between your monthly income and expenditure, delete your current chart, then select your total income cells in row 10 for all 12 months, including the heading. Now hold down the **Ctrl** key and select all the months in row 3 and the total expenses in row 19, including their row headings. Insert a chart as before, using the **Chart Wizard** button. Excel now displays a chart with your monthly income in blue and your expenses in purple.

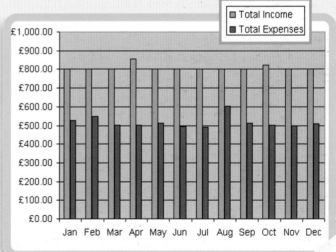

3 Remove your chart by selecting it and pressing the keyboard **Delete** key. To create a new chart with the month labels along the horizontal (X) axis, you need to give Excel more information. Select the cells in row 3 from 'Month' to 'Dec', then hold down the **Ctrl** key and click and drag to select your total expenses, including the heading as in Step 1. Click on the **Chart Wizard** button and then on the **Finish** button.

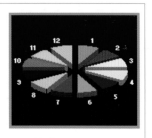
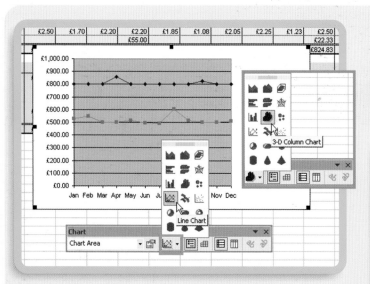

6 You can rotate 3-D charts to improve the viewing angle. Right-click on a blank area of chart and choose **3-D View** from the pop-up menu. When the dialogue box opens, use the arrow buttons to rotate the diagram. Click on the **Apply** button to see how your chart will look. Click on the **Default** button to revert to the original viewing angle.

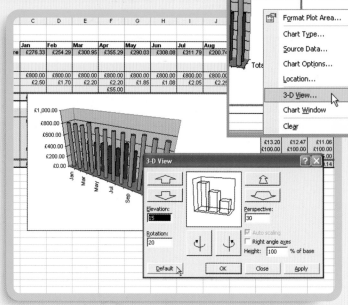

5 If you don't like the barchart format, or the type of data on your spreadsheet would be better represented using a different type of chart, you can choose a completely different style from a range of built-in chart templates. Click on your chart to display the **Chart** toolbar, and then click on the **Chart Type** button. To display your home finances, a simple Line Chart or 3-D Column Chart will work well. Simply select the chart type of your choice from the pop-up list and it will appear on screen.

Displaying Your Data

Grouping your data

Even with text and cell formatting, it can sometimes be difficult to track down the results of your calculations in a large spreadsheet. Excel's Group and Outline feature lets you group sections of data, and then switch instantly between displaying just the results of your calculations or the complete set of data in your spreadsheet.

SEE ALSO...
- *Columns and rows* p 34
- *Club database* p 78

BEFORE YOU START
*Open your family budget spreadsheet (see page 60) and save it under another name so you can safely use it to experiment with Excel's **Group and Outline** feature.*

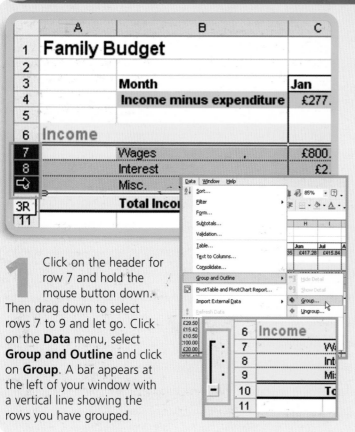

1 Click on the header for row 7 and hold the mouse button down. Then drag down to select rows 7 to 9 and let go. Click on the **Data** menu, select **Group and Outline** and click on **Group**. A bar appears at the left of your window with a vertical line showing the rows you have grouped.

2 Now select rows 13 to 18 in the 'Expenses' section and group these rows – another vertical line appears to the left of your data showing the new grouped rows. Check that you have grouped the rows between the section headings and the section totals. If not, use the **Undo** button on the **Standard** toolbar, or click on the **Edit** menu and choose **Undo** to go back.

	3	Month	
	4	Income minus expenditure	£277.08
	5		
	6	Income	
	7	Wages	£800.00
	8	Interest	£2.50
	9	Misc.	
	10	Total Income	£802.50
	11		
	12	Expenses	
	13	Mortgage/Rent	£350.00
	14	Gas	£29.50
	15	Electricity	£15.42
	16	Telephone	£10.50
	17	Food	£100.00
	18	Eating out	£20.00
	19	Total Expenses	£525.42
	20		
	21		

Expert advice

You can group columns as well as rows. Select the columns you want to group by clicking and dragging across their column headers. Then click on the **Data** menu, select **Group and Outline** and then click on **Group**.

Watch out

Unless your data is laid out in a consistent list format with similar entries next to each other, **Group and Outline** will hide the wrong rows. The summary rows should always be directly below or above the data rows.

1 2		A	B	C	D
	1	**Family Budget**			
	2				
	3		Month	Jan	Feb
	4		Income minus expenditure	£277.08	£399.29
	5				
	6	Income			
+	10		Total Income	£802.50	£801.70
	11				
	12	Expenses			
+	19		Total Expenses	£525.42	£402.41
	20				

1 2		A	B	C	D	E	F	M
	1	**Family Budget**						
	2							
	3		Month	Jan	Feb	Mar	Apr	M
	4		Income minus expenditure	£277.08	£399.29	£405.45	£461.29	
	5							
	6	Income						
	7		Wages	£800.00	£800.00	£800.00	£800.00	
	8		Interest	£2.50	£1.70	£2.20	£2.20	
	9		Misc.				£55.00	
	10		Total Income	£802.50	£801.70	£802.20	£857.20	
	11							

3 At the top of the new bar are two tiny buttons marked **1** and **2**. Click on the **1** button and your spreadsheet rows collapse to display only the section headings and the totals for each section. Click on the **2** button and the rows expand to fill their normal range. Use the small minus and plus buttons by each section to collapse and expand individual sections.

4 To remove groups one at a time, click **2** to expand the rows, select the rows you want to ungroup and click on the **Data** menu. Choose **Group and Outline** and select **Ungroup**. Alternatively, you can ungroup all in one go: select all your data by holding down **Ctrl** and pressing **A**, and then use the **Ungroup** command as before. If you print grouped and collapsed rows or columns, the hidden areas will not be printed.

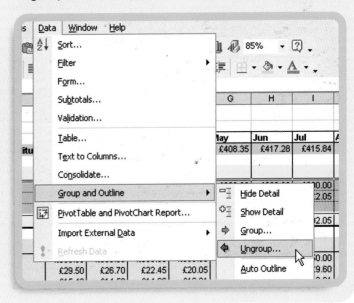

Freezing panes and splitting

One problem when scrolling down a large spreadsheet is that the column headings disappear from the top of the window. The same happens with row headings when you scroll to the right. Excel's Freeze Panes and Split features enable you to keep your headings in view and even display several sections of your spreadsheet at one time.

SEE ALSO...
● *Viewing options* p 88

BEFORE YOU START
Open your loan calculator (see page 56) and enter some data for *a loan that is to be repaid over a period of five years. Convert the '$' symbols to '£'s if necessary.*

1 To 'freeze' the rows above your columns of data, so that you can always see the column titles as you scroll down the page, first click in cell A18 just below your heading row. Then click on the **Window** menu and choose **Freeze Panes**. A thin line appears across the spreadsheet showing which sections have been frozen. Now, as you scroll down the page, the column headings will always be visible.

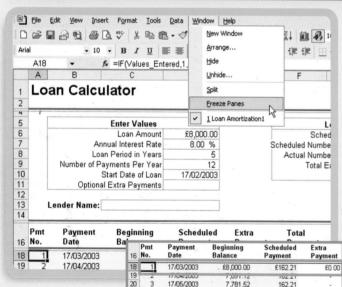

2 To 'unfreeze' the panes, click on the **Window** menu and select **Unfreeze Panes**. To freeze a range of columns and rows at the same time, click on the cell just below your headings row and to the right of the columns you want to freeze – in our example this is cell C18. Then click on the **Window** menu and choose **Freeze Panes**. You can now scroll across the spreadsheet and still see which row belongs to which payment date, and down the spreadsheet and still see your column headings.

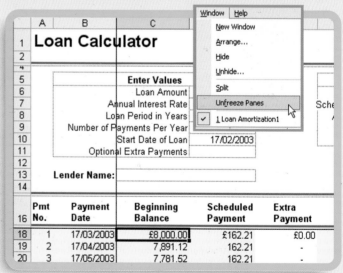

*Brighter idea!
Put copy of totals above — the headings*

That's amazing!

Excel includes a useful feature that enables you to make adjustments to numbers and see the results without having to scroll back and forth. Click on the **View** menu, choose **Toolbars** and select **Watch Window**. Click the **Add Watch** button and click the **Collapse Dialogue** button (with the red arrow) at the right. Then select the cell you want to 'watch' and click on **Add**. You can now make changes anywhere on your sheet and the results will appear in the **Watch Window**.

Bright idea

Instead of putting column totals at the bottom of your columns, put them above your column headings. This way, as long as they are frozen, they will stay visible as you scroll down the window and enter more data.

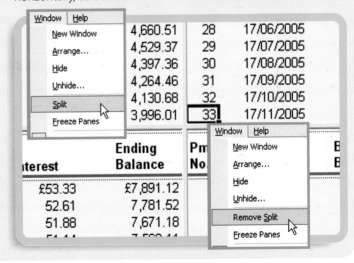

4 To split the window horizontally, click on the **Split Box** next to the arrow at the right of the horizontal scroll bar. Drag it across the screen to position it. You can move the splits at any time by dragging them. If you then want to split the screen vertically as well as horizontally, select the cell before which you want the split, click on the **Window** menu and choose **Split**. Drag the splits to move them. Now you can view up to four sections of your spreadsheet at one time. To remove the splits, click on the **Window** menu and choose **Remove Split**. Note that you can't split the window when it is frozen.

3 If you want to work on two separate areas of your worksheet, you can split the window either vertically or horizontally. This creates independent views, in which you can scroll around and enter data. To split the window vertically, click on the **Split Box** above the up arrow at the top of the right vertical scroll bar and drag it down. This creates two windows and you can work in either.

Sort your data

Whether you are using a spreadsheet to store a list of items or to calculate your monthly expenditure, it is useful to organise the information with the dates in order and any names or descriptions alphabetically listed. To save time and effort, Excel has a powerful sort feature, which carefully rearranges your data in ascending or descending order.

BEFORE YOU START
Set up a spreadsheet listing details of your friends and relatives under the headings, 'Surname', 'First Name' and 'Birthday'. Add a border under the headings (see page 50).

1 To sort your new database of birthdays by date, click anywhere in the column of dates to select a single cell. Then click on the **Data** menu and choose **Sort**. When the **Sort** dialogue box opens, make sure the 'Header row' option under **My list has** is selected. Excel automatically selects your 'Birthday' column under **Sort by**.

2 To sort your list in ascending date order – with the earliest dates at the top of the list – make sure the 'Ascending' option is selected and click the **OK** button. You can reverse this by clicking the **Undo** button on the **Standard** toolbar. To sort your data with the most recent date at the top of the list, open the **Sort** dialogue box again, select the 'Descending' option and click on **OK**.

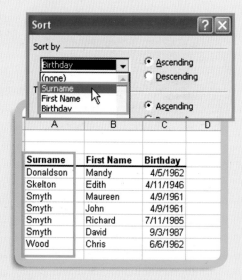

3 Excel automatically assumes that the column in which you initially clicked is the one you want to use for the sort. But you can select any of your columns from the drop-down list under **Sort by**. Try selecting 'Surname' then click on **OK**. Your list is now sorted alphabetically by surname. You can do the same by first name.

Watch out
If you have applied formatting, such as borders and cell colours, to your list you will find they are moved with the data when you perform the sort. Keep fills and borders in your lists simple and avoid row gaps because Excel will put them at the bottom of the list when it sorts.

Expert advice
If the data you want to sort has no column headings, or the headings are not directly above the rows you want to sort, select the 'No header row' option under **My list has** in the **Sort** dialogue box. You can then select the letter of the column by which you want to sort from the drop-down list under **Sort by**.

5 Your list will now be sorted by surname first and then by birthday. This means any people who share a surname will be listed first in alphabetical order and then by their birthday. If your list contained people who shared the same birthday and surname, you could sort your list by a third criteria, so that people are sorted by surname alphabetically, then birthday, then first name alphabetically.

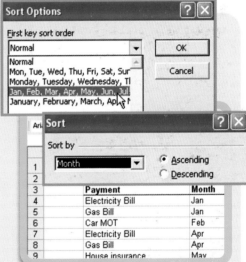

4 If your list contains family members who share the same surname, you can sort your list by two criteria. For example, you could sort by surname and then by birthday. Click anywhere in your list and open the **Sort** dialogue box. Select 'Surname' under **Sort by** and 'Birthday' under the first **Then by**. Select the 'Ascending' option under **Sort by** and the 'Descending' option under **Then by** and click on **OK**.

6 If your data contains the names of months, you can instruct Excel to sort them in month order instead of alphabetically. Click in the 'Month' column, open the **Sort** dialogue box and click on the **Options** button. Under **First key sort order** choose the list that matches your data and click on **OK**. Make sure 'Month' is selected under **Sort by** and click on **OK**.

Using AutoFilter

Excel's AutoFilter tool can pick out entries from your data that meet specific criteria. For instance, if you have a list of your accounts and want to view only the 'Electricity' entries, Excel can temporarily hide the other items. This process does not affect your data or any calculations on your spreadsheet – it simply displays the items that you have chosen to see.

BEFORE YOU START
Enter 'Date', 'Description' and 'Amount' in columns A, B and C.

Enter data under each heading and repeat a few descriptions, such as 'Electricity', in the list.

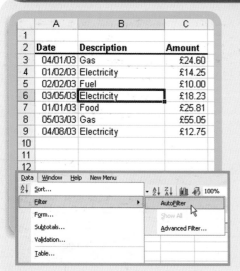

1 Select any cell in your list, then click on the **Data** menu and choose **Filter**. From the submenu that pops up, choose **AutoFilter**. Excel adds a downward arrow button to the right of every heading cell. When you click on an arrow, a drop-down list appears containing entries for all the items in that particular column.

2 Click on the arrow to the right of 'Description'. From the list, choose the item you want to isolate, for example 'Electricity'. Excel immediately hides all the other entries in the list and groups all the 'Electricity' entries in the 'Description' column at the top of the spreadsheet, making it easy to analyse those items. The arrow turns blue to show your list is filtered.

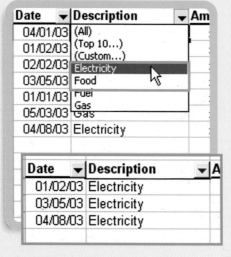

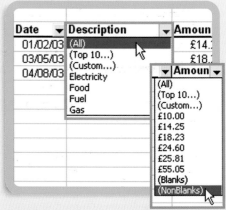

3 To restore your data, click on the blue downward arrow to the right of 'Description' and choose '(All)' from the list. You can also isolate any rows where the cell in your selected column is blank; this is useful for finding rows in your data where you have forgotten to enter a description. If you want to display only those rows that have an amount in them, for example, and ignore rows containing amounts you have yet to fill in, then use the '(NonBlanks)' option.

Watch out
If you have been inconsistent in the way you typed data in a column – for example, 'Electricity' and 'Elec.' – Excel will create separate entries for these on the **AutoFilter** list. This means you will not be able to filter all your electricity entries in one go. Make sure you always use the same spelling for identical items in a list.

Bright idea
If you no longer want to use the AutoFilter *feature, click on the* Data *menu and choose* Filter. *Then click on* AutoFilter *to remove the tick from next to it and turn off the* AutoFilter *arrows.*

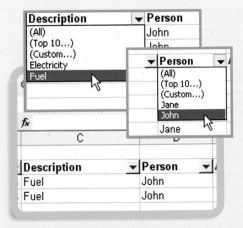

5 The 'Custom' item that appears on each drop-down list enables you to perform some smart filters. You can isolate all items in a list beginning with a certain character, or which are equal to, greater than, or less than a specific value. To isolate all bills greater than £30, for example, choose 'Custom' and select 'is greater than' from the 'Amount' list. Then enter '30' in the box to the right and click on **OK**.

4 You can isolate data that matches two different sets of criteria by applying two **AutoFilters**. For instance, if your spreadsheet had fuel entries and you had a 'Person' column indicating who had incurred each expense, you could select 'Fuel' from your 'Description' drop-down list and then choose a name from the 'Person' list. Excel will show only those fuel payments made by the selected person.

6 We can now use this custom filter together with another filter to identify all electricity bills over £30. Click the downward arrow to the right of 'Description' and choose 'Electricity'. Excel combines the two filters and displays the requested data. If you wanted, you could even tell Excel only to display electricity payments over £30 paid by a specific person, by selecting a name from the drop-down list next to 'Person'.

Club database

Every database, whether it holds your medical notes at your doctor's surgery or details of flights on the Internet, stores its data in a table that looks like a spreadsheet. You can use Excel as a simple database to store lists of information such as details of club members. You can even sort your data by name or date and use a window called a Form to input and locate entries.

SEE ALSO...
● *Style your data* p 44
● *Drawing in Excel* p 64
● *Sort your data* p 74

BEFORE YOU START
Open a new spreadsheet and type 'Club Membership' in cell A1. Format it as bold and choose '16' from the **Font Size** menu and 'Century Gothic' from the **Font** menu.

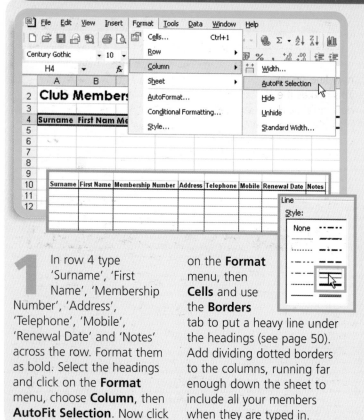

1 In row 4 type 'Surname', 'First Name', 'Membership Number', 'Address', 'Telephone', 'Mobile', 'Renewal Date' and 'Notes' across the row. Format them as bold. Select the headings and click on the **Format** menu, choose **Column**, then **AutoFit Selection**. Now click on the **Format** menu, then **Cells** and use the **Borders** tab to put a heavy line under the headings (see page 50). Add dividing dotted borders to the columns, running far enough down the sheet to include all your members when they are typed in.

2 Format the headings as a dark colour using the **Font Color** palette on the **Formatting** toolbar. Widen both the 'Notes' and the 'Address' columns by dragging their column header boundaries (see page 34). Then change the colour of the 'Notes' column to light yellow using the **Fill Color** palette. Select the D header and click on the **Format** menu, then **Cells** and choose the **Alignment** tab. Put a tick next to **Wrap text** under **Text control** and click on **OK**. This means that when you enter addresses, the cells will automatically expand to fit.

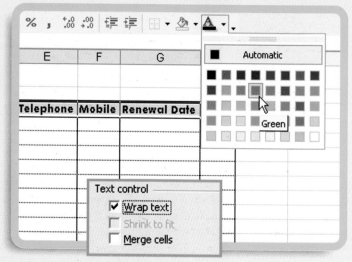

Bright idea
Hold down Alt **on your keyboard and press** Return **to start a new line within a cell. This is useful for entering addresses and saves you having to format the cell as 'Wrap text'. Note that you cannot use this technique with Forms.**

Records and fields
A record is an entry in a database made up of categories of information called 'Fields'. In a database of contact details, each person would have one record, containing name, address and telephone fields. In Excel, each row of data is one record and each cell in a row is a field. The column headings are called field names.

Record | Field

7	Surname	First Name	Membership Numbe
8	Smyth	James	1234
9	Jameson	Janice	5432

3 Now you are ready to start entering your data. Click on cell A4, which contains the word 'Surname', and then click on the **Data** menu followed by **Form**. Click on **OK** in the warning box and Excel will display a window that you can use to enter data quickly. Type your first member's surname in the top box – known as a

field – and press the **Tab** key to move to the next field. Type in the member's first name and then use the **Tab** key to move to 'Membership Number'. Continue to add data until the record for that member is complete. Then click on the **New** button and enter the next member's details. Click on **Close** when you have finished.

4 Each time you click on the **New** or **Close** buttons, Excel inserts the data from your form into a new line on your spreadsheet. This makes it easier to enter data quickly. However, it is possible to type directly into your spreadsheet if you prefer – you can use the **Tab** key to move across the row and the arrow keys to move down. If you use this method, Excel's

AutoComplete tool will help you to enter repeated data by popping up suggestions based on what you've already typed. Press **Return** to accept the suggestion as soon as it appears or keep typing to enter new data. You can also enter repeated data by right-clicking a cell, choosing **Pick From List** and clicking on the item you want from the pop-up list.

Watch out
If you have applied borders under your headings and then use the **Form** window to input data, Excel automatically applies these borders between each new record. To instruct Excel to add your own borders when you use the form, apply them to the data when you've finished entering a couple of records, then open and use the form again.

Bright idea
You can sort your club members by any of the column headings (see page 74). Click anywhere in the list of members, then click on the Data menu and choose Sort.

Sheet1   ? X

		1 of 5
Surname:	Smyth	New
First Name:	James	Delete
Membership Number:	12345	Restore
Address:	10 Acacia Avenue, Boreha	
Telephone:	020 8888 1234	Find Prev
Mobile:	07900 000111	Find Next
Renewal Date:	10/4/2003	Criteria
Notes:		Close

6 To delete records from your database, select a cell in your list and open the **Form** window. Then use the **Criteria** button to locate the record you want to delete, or simply work through the records using the **Find Next** and **Find Prev** buttons.

Click on the **Delete** button and then click **OK** in the warning box. The selected record will be deleted. You can also delete a record in the spreadsheet by clicking on the row header for the record you want to delete and clicking on the **Edit** menu, then **Delete**.

Sheet1   ? X

		2 of 5
Surname:	Jameson	New
First Name:	Ronnie	Delete
Membership Number:	56789	Restore
Address:	15 Dustwood Drive, Barne	
Telephone:	020 888 0000	Find Prev
Mobile:	07900 000111	Find Next
		Criteria
		Close

Microsoft Excel   X

⚠ Displayed record will be permanently deleted.

OK   Cancel

5 You can use the **Form** window to quickly find entries in your database that match specific criteria. For example, if you had a phone number but no name, you could locate the entry instantly by using the **Criteria** button.

Just select a cell anywhere in your data, click on the **Data** menu and choose **Form**. Then click on the **Criteria** button and enter the data for which you are searching. Finally click on the **Find Next** button until the record appears.

Customising Excel

Change your preferences

Once you have built up some experience with Excel you will want to modify its settings to suit your way of working. From hiding gridlines to fine-tuning your edit options, Excel helps you work more efficiently by allowing you to control its appearance and response to your actions. And you can set up a password to protect your work and settings.

SEE ALSO...
- *Explore the program p 16*
- *Save your work p 22*
- *Cut copy and paste p 32*

APPEARANCE AND EDITING
Click on the Tools **menu and then choose** Options **to access Excel's preferences. These are arranged by category under different tabs.**

Viewing options
The **View** tab provides you with options to change the way the Excel window looks. Here you can turn the gridlines on and off – this is useful if you have created borders to act as guidelines – and choose not to display zero values in the results of calculations.

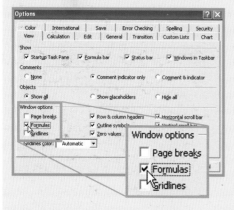

If you want to check every formula in your spreadsheet, put a tick next to 'Formulas' under **Window options** and click on **OK**. All the

formulas will then be displayed so you can quickly see any errors. Remove the tick to restore your spreadsheet and display the results of its calculations. Other options control the appearance of the scrollbars, column and row headers, and also the colour of the gridlines.

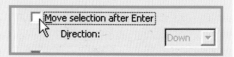

Editing options
Click on the **Edit** tab to modify the way Excel responds to your actions. By default, Excel allows you to edit cells by double-clicking. If you don't like this method you can switch it off by removing the tick from next to 'Edit directly in cell'.

Also, some people prefer to disable the drag and drop feature, which allows you to move a range of cells by dragging it to a new location. If you don't like Excel moving the cell pointer down when you press **Return**, or **Enter**, you can turn that option off by removing the tick next to

'Move selection after Enter'. Or, if you want Excel to move the cell pointer to the cell to the right, left or above the current cell when you press the **Return** or **Enter** key, leave the tick in place and choose the preferred option from the drop-down list next to 'Direction'.

Two further tick boxes on the **Edit** tab panel allow you to choose whether Excel helps you with special options when you paste or insert data. If you want to see the helpful pop-up lists, make sure there's a tick in both boxes.

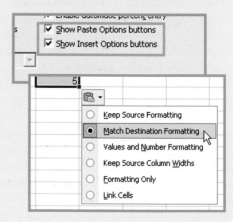

Close up
Put a tick next to 'Extend list formats and formulas' on the Edit *tab if you want Excel to automatically format new items you add to a list in the same way as the preceding items. Excel will also then copy down any formulas that are repeated in every row.*

Background error checking
If a small green triangle appears in a cell, this means background error checking is enabled. This monitors your work and warns of possible problems in a pop-up tip box. To turn it off, go to the **Options** menu, click on the **Error Checking** tab and untick 'Enable background error checking'.

GENERAL CONTROLS

There are several options on the General **tab of the** Options **window – some of the most commonly used items are outlined below.**

Settings

Under the **General** tab you can set the standard font that is used when Excel starts up (normally Arial 10pt) and

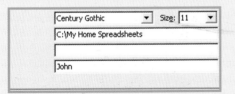

change the default save location. This is the folder on your hard disk that Excel chooses when you first save. Other options include turning on and off the **Function tooltips** that pop up when the mouse pointer hovers over a button, and turning on and off

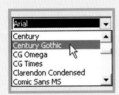

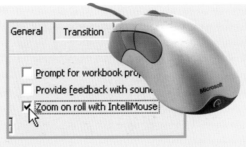

sound feedback for certain actions and errors. You can even opt to use the wheel (if you have one) on your mouse to zoom in and out of your spreadsheet instead of scrolling.

The number next to 'Recently used file list' controls the number of recently accessed files that appear when you open the **Task Pane**, or which are listed at the bottom of the **File** menu. You can access up to nine of your most recently opened files by a single click in the **Task Pane** or **File** menu – the default is four.

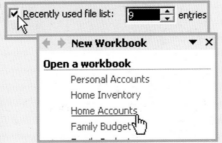

ADDED SECURITY

To keep a spreadsheet safe from prying eyes, you can set up a password, which must be entered in order to open the document.

Password protection

Click on the **Security** tab, enter a memorable password in the box next to **Password to open** under 'File encryption settings for this workbook' and click on **OK**. Excel asks you to retype the password to make sure it is stored correctly. The next time your spreadsheet is

opened, the password must be entered before it can be viewed. Passwords are case-sensitive. This means you must type them using the correct combination of upper and lower-case letters you used when creating the password. Make sure the **Caps Lock** is not switched on when you enter a password.

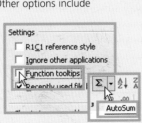

Change menus and toolbars

Excel's toolbars and menus are completely customisable – you can add or remove any command, and move buttons and menu items around to suit your needs. You can even change the images on buttons to make them more user-friendly or create new toolbars and menus from scratch so that all the functions you use most often are grouped together.

SEE ALSO...
- *Explore the program* p 16
- *Recording a macro* p 96

BEFORE YOU START
*Working with toolbars is easier if your **Standard** and **Formatting*** *toolbars do not share one line. See page 13 to position the toolbars on two lines.*

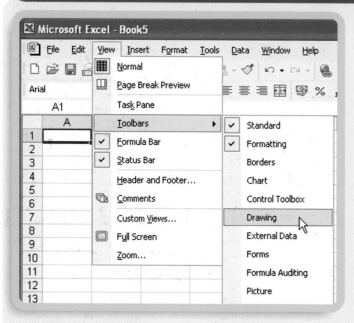

1 To view or hide any of Excel's built-in toolbars, click on the **View** menu, choose **Toolbars** and select the item you want to display or hide. Toolbars that are already displayed have a tick next to them. When they are enabled, some toolbars will be attached (or docked) to the top of the screen by default, and some will be free-floating.

2 Each toolbar has a selection of buttons. You can quickly add or remove individual buttons by clicking the small downward arrow to the right of a toolbar and clicking on **Add or Remove Buttons**, followed by the name of the toolbar you want to modify. Then use the tick list to choose the buttons you want to see.

Key word
Commands are instructions you give Excel via a menu item or toolbar button. Using the Customize dialogue box, you can assign any command to any menu or toolbar.

Close up
If you want to move or remove a button or menu item quickly, press and hold down the Alt key and drag the item to its new location, or anywhere in the middle of the spreadsheet window to remove it.

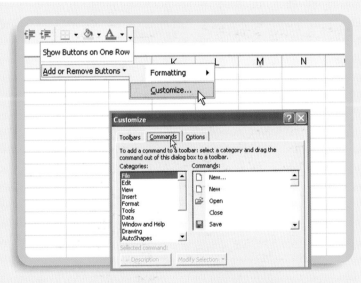

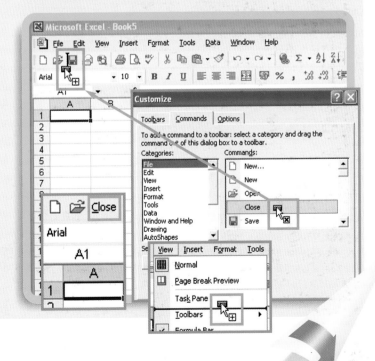

4 Click on an item in the list under **Categories** to display all that category's commands in the panel on the right. Then drag a command onto a toolbar. For example, click on **File** from the **Categories** list, then drag **Close** from the **Commands** list to the **Standard** toolbar and let go. Similarly, to add a command to a menu, drag it over the menu item and then down the menu as it opens.

3 If you want to add **commands** to your menus or buttons to your toolbars, click on the small downward arrow to the right of any toolbar, select **Add or Remove Buttons** and **Customize** from the pop-up menus and then choose the **Commands** tab. You'll see the commands organised in categories. Be careful while this dialogue box is open as it is easy to make changes by mistake. If things do go wrong, you can reset your toolbars and menus – see Resetting toolbars, page 86.

Resetting toolbars
You can reset your toolbars to Excel's default settings by opening the **Customize** dialogue box, clicking the **Toolbars** tab, selecting each toolbar and clicking the **Reset** button followed by **OK**. Reset your menus by right-clicking on each while the **Customize** box is open and choosing **Reset** from the pop-up menu.

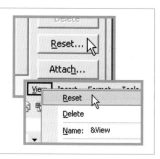

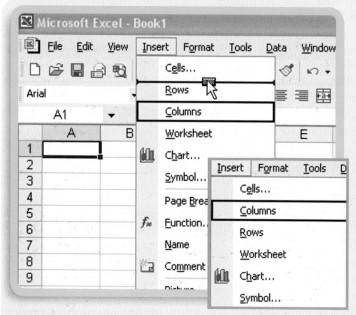

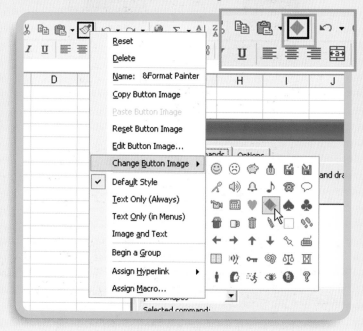

6 You can edit each menu item and toolbar button individually. While the **Customize** window is open, right-click on a button, or click once to open a menu and right-click on an item to edit it. From the pop-up list you can change menu names, edit or modify button images, or even change buttons to text.

5 While the **Customize** window is open, you can move any existing menu item or toolbar button by clicking on it and dragging it to a new location. A vertical black line indicates where the item will be positioned when you let go of the mouse button. In this example, we have just swapped **Rows** with **Columns** on the **Insert** menu, but it is also possible to move items onto different menus.

Expert advice
If you find that you often forget what a button does, you can add text to the button. Right-click on a toolbar and choose **Customize**. Then right-click on the button you want to change and select **Image and Text** from the pop-up list. Choose **Text Only** if you don't want to see the button image at all.

Close up
If you're unsure of the function of an item on the Commands *list in the* Customize *dialogue box, select the item and then click on* Description *to see a short description.*

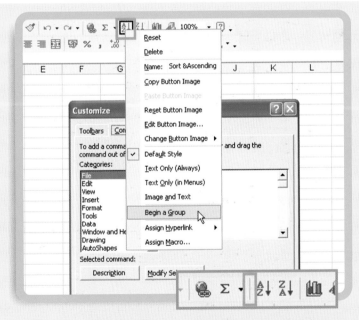

8 To create a new toolbar, open the **Customize** box and click on the **Toolbars** tab. Click the **New** button, choose a name for your toolbar and click **OK**. Then click the **Commands** tab and drag the tools you want from the list on the right to your new toolbar. Click **Close** when you've finished. Open your new toolbar by clicking on the **View** menu, choosing **Toolbars** and selecting its name. To create a new menu, scroll down the **Categories** list under the **Commands** tab and locate **New Menu**. Drag **New Menu** from the **Commands** list to your **Menu** bar. Select a category and drag commands to your menu. Name your new menu and click on **Close**.

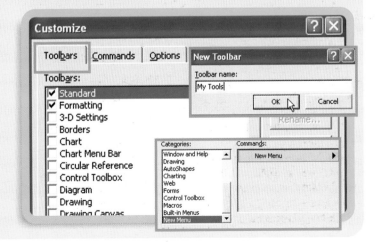

7 You can place a divider line before a button or above a menu item to help to visually separate tools that perform different functions. Simply right-click on an item and select **Begin a Group**. To delete a divider line between two buttons or menu items, first open the **Customize** box and then drag the buttons or menu items closer together. Then click on the **Close** button.

Viewing options

It is sometimes necessary to change the size of the viewable area of your spreadsheet. This can make it easier to enter data, or to format cells and text. The Zoom function enables you to enlarge or reduce your view of the data without affecting the way the spreadsheet prints. You can choose from a series of preset zooms, or just type in your own percentage.

SEE ALSO...
● *Explore the program* p 16
● *Freezing panes and splitting* p 72

ZOOMING AROUND

If your family budget spreadsheet overflows your computer screen by a few columns or rows, you can zoom out to save scrolling up and down or from left to right.

Zoom box

Use the **Zoom** drop-down list on the **Standard** toolbar to quickly change the size of your view. There are six options on the list. Zoom to 200% if you want to examine a series of cells close up, or to 75% if you want to see more of your spreadsheet on the screen. Use the **Selection** option to fit a selected area of the spreadsheet into the Excel window. If none of the built-in settings suit your worksheet, you can type your own value in the box – choose any amount between 10% and 400% and press the **Return** key to confirm the change.

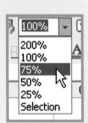

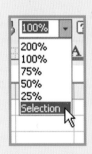

Custom views

If, for example, you find yourself viewing one part of your spreadsheet at 100% zoom and you want to view another section at 50% zoom, you can set up custom views. These allow you to quickly switch between sections of your spreadsheet at different zoom levels.

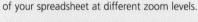

Set up the zoom level and the range of cells you want to see, and click on the **View** menu then **Custom Views**. Click the **Add** button, type a name for your view next to **Name** in the **Add View** dialogue box and click **OK**. Then move to the second range of cells, select your zoom level and add another custom view with a different name. Now you can switch instantly between your views by clicking on the **View** menu and then **Custom Views**, selecting your new view and clicking on the **Show** button.

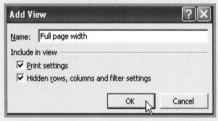

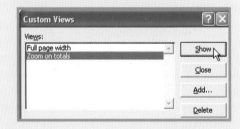

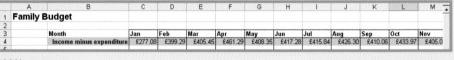

100% zoom

85% zoom (custom setting)

Excel's Advanced Features

Advanced functions

Excel has more than 200 built-in functions, organised in nine categories, which range from AutoSum, covered earlier in this book, to functions that are used to carry out complex statistical and mathematical calculations. While you may never need some of these powerful tools, there are many handy functions that you can use to build advanced spreadsheets.

SEE ALSO...
- *Using AutoSum p 26*
- *Cut, copy and paste p 32*
- *Columns and rows p 34*
- *Style your data p 44*

BEFORE YOU START
*Open your club database (see page 78) and select column H – the 'Notes' column. Click on the **Insert** menu and choose **Column**. Name your new column 'Overdue'.*

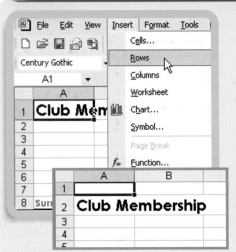

1 Excel's **IF** function checks to see whether a certain condition is met, and returns a value for true and a value for false. Here we will use the **IF** function to check the members' renewal dates against the current date, and to display a visual reminder if the fee is overdue. First, select cell A1, click on the **Insert** menu and choose **Rows** to put a blank row above your title.

2 Click on the **Insert Function** button to the left of the **Formula Bar**. When the **Insert Function** dialogue box opens, choose 'Date & Time' from the drop-down list to the right of **Or select a category** and scroll down to 'TODAY' in the list under **Select a function**. Click on **OK** and then on **OK** in the **Function Arguments** box. The current date is inserted in cell A1.

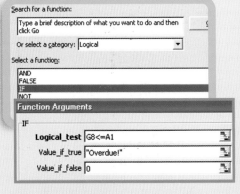

3 Click in the top cell in your new 'Overdue' column. Open the **Insert Function** dialogue box and choose 'Logical' from the **Or select a category** list. Then select 'IF' from the list underneath and click on **OK**. When the **Function Arguments** box opens, click on the top cell in the 'Renewal Date' column on your spreadsheet. Then, in the dialogue box, type '<=A1' in the box next to 'Logical_test'. Click in the box to the right of 'Value_if_true' and type 'Overdue!', then type '0' next to 'Value_if_false' and click on **OK**.

Watch out
If you see the message '#REF!' or '#VALUE' in a cell, you have either entered the formula incorrectly, or copied and pasted a formula that refers to a cell incorrectly. Double-click the cell containing the problem formula and click on each section in turn to make sure you have selected the correct reference cells.

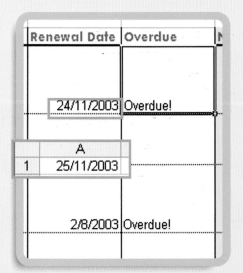

5 Before you copy this formula down the 'Overdue' column, you want to be sure Excel always refers to cell A1. If you simply copied and pasted the formula, Excel would move the reference down one cell for each new copy – to A2, A3, A4 and so on. To 'fix' the reference, edit the cell containing your **IF** function. Add a '$' before both the A and the 1 in 'A1' so it reads '$A$1'. Now copy and paste the formula down the 'Overdue' column.

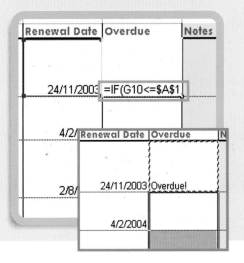

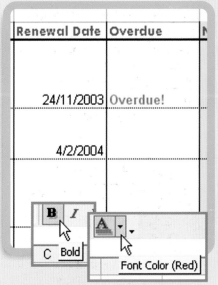

4 Excel now compares the value in the 'Renewal' column with the current date in cell A1 and displays 'Overdue!' if the renewal date is earlier or the same. Otherwise, '0' will be displayed. Click on the **Tools** menu, select **Options** and choose the **View** tab to hide zero values so the column either displays 'Overdue!' or a blank cell.

6 It is helpful to format these 'Overdue' reminders so that they stand out. Select the 'Overdue' column except for its heading and format it as bold and red text. Now, when a membership is up for renewal you'll see a red 'Overdue!' reminder next to that person's name.

COMMONLY USED FUNCTIONS

To insert a function, click on the
Insert Function **button on the**
Formula **toolbar. Choose 'All'**
next to Or select a category **and select**
the desired function from the list
under Select a function. **You can type**
the first letter of the function to move
quickly down the list. Click on OK **to**
open the Function Arguments **box.**

AVERAGE

This function calculates the average of a series
of numbers. Its arguments can be a range of
adjacent cells, such as B3:B6, a series of cell
references separated by commas – B3, B5, A9 –
or simply the numbers you wish to average. For
example, if you type '=AVERAGE(4,4,5,7)' into a
cell the function returns the value '5'.

	A3	▼		*fx* =AVERAGE(A5:A11)
	A	B	C	D
1	**Fuel Consumption**			
2				
3	28.67			
4	**MPG**			
5	24.20			
6	29.00			
7	23.60			
8	25.00			
9	33.04			
10	42.00			
11	23.85			
12				
13				
14				
15				

MAX

It can be difficult to scan through a long list
of figures looking for the highest value, for
example, a list of quiz scores. Excel's **MAX**
function locates the largest value in a range
of cells and inserts it in the cell in which
the function is entered. For example,
'=MAX(B5:B10)' returns the highest value
from the range B5 to B10.

	B12	▼		*fx* =MAX(B5:B10)
	A		B	C
1	**Quiz Results**			
2				
3				
4	**Name**		**Score**	
5	Jacob Myers		23	
6	Jackie Glover		44	
7	Michael Smith		51	
8	Michael Tate		22	
9	Frank Horner		84	
10	Maureen Taylor		86	
11				
12	**Highest Score**		**86**	✛
13				

ROUND

Excel's sophisticated calculations are capable of
producing results to a great number of decimal
places. However, you may want to round all
your results up to two places, for instance, in an
area calculation. The **ROUND** function allows
you to specify a number or a cell reference and
the number of decimal places you want to
round up to, which is usually 2. For example,
'=ROUND(12.567,2)' rounds up 12.567 to

12.57. You can refer to cells too –
'=ROUND(B3/A9,3)' divides the value in B3
by the value in A9 and rounds up the result to
3 decimal places. A zero after the comma will
cause Excel to round up to a whole number –
thus, '=ROUND(12.568,0)' would give the result
'13'. Note that formatting the cell as currency to
two decimal places will round up the value too.

	D5	▼		*fx* =ROUND(B5*C5,2)	
	A	B	C	D	E
	Room sizes				
	Room	Length	Width	Area	
	Lounge	20.23	15.94	322.47	
	Kitchen	10.25	11.53	118.18	

RANK

The **RANK** function finds the ranked position of
a number in a list of numbers. This is useful for
exam marking or sports events. If you have a
column of numbers starting at B5 and ending at
B10, enter '=RANK(B5,$B$5:$B$10)' in cell C5.
Then copy and paste the formula into cells C6
to C10 to rank all the numbers in the column.

	C5	▼		*fx* =RANK(B5,$B$5:$B$10)
	A		B	C
1	**Quiz Results**			
2				
3				
4	**Name**		**Score**	**Rank**
5	Jacob Myers		23	5
6	Jackie Glover		44	
7	Michael Smith		51	
8	Michael Tate			
9	Frank Horner			
10	Maureen Taylor			
11				

Score	**Rank**
23	5
44	4
51	3
22	6
84	2
86	1

Help on functions
Try clicking on each of the functions in
the **Insert Function** dialogue box and
then clicking the blue **Help on this**
function link at the bottom left of the
box. Excel's **Help** window will open,
offering comprehensive assistance on
the selected function and examples of
how it is commonly used.

NOT
OR
TRUE

IF(logical_test,value_if_true,v...
Checks whether a condition is met, a...
another value if FALSE.

Help on this function

Close up
Note that if two results are
the same, RANK gives them
the same ranking and skips
the next position. For example, if there are
two 5th positions there will be no 6th.

PMT

Calculating loan repayments can be difficult, but Excel can do this for you with its **PMT** function. There are three arguments: the interest rate, the number of payments for the loan and the value. A simple example to work out the monthly payments on a loan of £8000 over 5 years at 9.5% annual interest would read: '=PMT(9.5%/12,60,8000)'. The 9.5% is divided by 12 to get the monthly interest rate, which is then multiplied by the number of months (60) and the amount. You could create a mini spreadsheet so you can enter the amount, interest rate and period in separate cells and have Excel calculate the result for you.

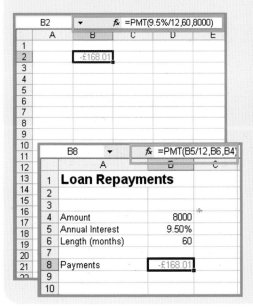

SUMIF

The **SUMIF** function adds the values in a list that match certain conditions. For instance, this function can be used to extract values in an accounts database that have a specific description next to them – for example, 'Gas' or 'Electricity' – and add them together, allowing you to see exactly how much you have spent on each type of expenditure. There are three arguments: the range containing the items you want to be evaluated, the criteria, and the range containing the amounts.

	A	B	C
1	**Accounts**		
2		Total:	£202.25
3	Date	Item	Amount
4	02/01/2004	Gas	£10.00
5	03/01/2004	Electricity	£15.00
6	09/02/2004	Fuel	£20.00
7	15/02/2004	Fuel	£12.00
8	10/03/2004	Gas	£25.00
9	15/03/2004	Electricity	£40.00
10	17/03/2004	Fuel	£20.00
11	25/03/2004	Fuel	£25.50
12	19/06/2004	Gas	£15.75
13	21/06/2004	Electricity	£19.00

fx =SUMIF($B$4:$B$13,"Gas",$C$4:$C$13)

Breakdown		
Gas	Electricity	Fuel
£50.75	£74.00	£77.50

In our example, the range B4 to B13 is to be evaluated and the criteria are 'Gas', 'Electricity' and 'Fuel'. The final range in the formula is C4 to C13, which contains the amounts to be added up.

RAND

If you want to generate random numbers, for instance, to play in a lottery game, Excel's **RAND** function can be used. In its basic form – '=RAND()' – the function generates numbers between 0 and 1. To create a quick lottery number generator, which supplies numbers between 1 and 50, the formula '=RAND()*(49-1)+1' should be entered into six adjacent cells. Every time the F9 key is pressed, a new series of numbers is created.

	A	B	C	D	E	F
1	**Lottery Number Generator**					
2						
3						
4	1	2	3	4	5	6
5	21	8	23	45	38	16

fx =RAND()*(49-1)+1

TODAY

The function '=TODAY()' tells you the current date. This is useful if you want to compare a deadline with the current date and return a warning if the deadline has passed.

A1		*fx* =TODAY()		
	A	B	C	D
1	23/12/04			

Saving money using PMT

You can use the **PMT** function to work out how much to save each month to achieve a certain amount. For example, '=PMT(6%/12,18*12,0,50000)' returns the value of '-£129.08' in order to save £50,000 at an annual interest rate of 6% over 18 years, or 216 monthly payments.

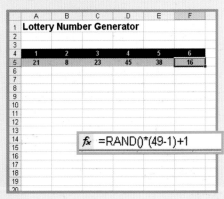

Time calculations

A special format is required for times and dates in Excel because, behind the scenes, the program uses standard decimal numbers to calculate with this data. If you want to carry out calculations using times and dates, Excel's Format Cells dialogue box includes options to help you. You can format a cell as a date, time or a combination of both.

SEE ALSO...
- *Excel formulas* p 24
- *Advanced functions* p 90

BEFORE YOU START
In this example we will construct a spreadsheet that uses time formatting to allow the user to keep track of how many hours they have spent on a project.

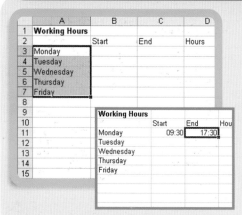

1 Open a blank spreadsheet, type a title in cell A1 and make it bold. Type column headings into row 2, as above, and type 'Monday' in cell A3. Then click on the bottom right-hand corner of this cell and drag the **Fill Handle** down to cell A7. Excel enters the days into the cells automatically. Type in a start and end time in the format 'hh:mm', for example, '9:30' and '17:30'. Excel recognises this is a time and formats the cell as soon as you press **Return** to confirm your entry.

2 You can now enter a formula that will subtract your start time from your end time to calculate the number of hours and minutes worked. Click in cell D3 and type '=IF(C3>0,C3-B3,0)' then press **Return**. This formula will only subtract your start time from your end time once an end time is entered. Select the range from D1 to D7 and click on the **Format** menu. Then choose **Cells** and click on the **Number** tab. Select 'Custom' from the Category list and the 'hh:mm' option from the **Type** list. Click on **OK**.

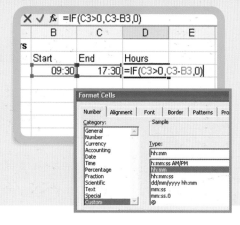

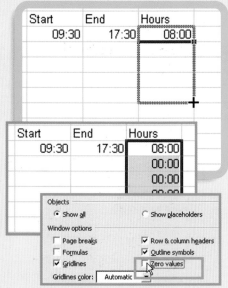

3 Use the fill handle to copy the formula from D3 down to D7. If you don't want to see the zeros you can click on the **Tools** menu, choose **Options** and click on the **View** tab. Then remove the tick from next to 'Zero values' and click on **OK**.

Close up
This example uses an 'IF' function rather than simply subtracting the start time from the end time because, until you 'clock out', the result of the subtraction is negative and Excel displays '####' if it sees a negative time.

Calculating dates
If you want to work out what the date will be, say, four weeks (28 days) after the current date, insert the current date in cell B2 by pressing the **Ctrl** and **;** keys simultaneously. Then, in C2, type '=B2+28' and press **Return**. Excel adds 28 days to the date in B2 and displays it in C2. Excel chooses the date format automatically.

	10		**B**	*I*	U
▼			*fx*	=B2+28	

	B	C
	20/12/2003	17/01/2004

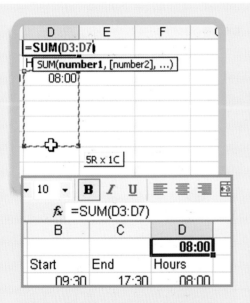

	D	E	F	
	=SUM(D3:D7)			
	SUM(**number1**, [number2], ...)			
	08:00			
			5R x 1C	

	10		**B**	*I*	U	≡ ≡ ≡

fx =SUM(D3:D7)

	B	C	D
			08:00
	Start	End	Hours
	09:30	17:30	08:00

4 To add all your daily total hours together, click on cell D1 and then click on the **AutoSum** button. Select the range from D3 to D7 and press **Return**. This adds together all the results of the formulas in column D to calculate the weekly total hours. Format this cell as bold.

5 Now you can start to enter the rest of your data from a timesheet, or as you arrive and leave each day. Type in your entries in the 'hh:mm' format as before. If you want to 'clock in', you can insert the current time in the 'Start' column quickly by pressing the **Ctrl**, **Shift** and the **;** keys together. Repeat this in the 'End' column when you are ready to 'clock out'.

	A	B	C	D
1	Working Hours			1
2		Start	End	Hours
3	Monday	09:30	17:30	0
4	Tuesday	09:30	17:30	0
5	Wednesday	09:30	18:30	0
6	Thursday	10:00	18:00	0
7	Friday	09:45	19:15	0
8				
9				
10				
11				
12				
13				
14				
15				
16				
17				

Ctrl   ⇧

	A	B	C	D
1	Working Hours			18:30
2	Week1	Start	End	Hours
3	Monday	09:30	17:30	08:00
4	Tuesday	09:30	17:30	08:00
5	Wednesday	09:30	18:30	09:00
6	Thursday	10:00	18:00	08:00
7	Friday	09:45	19:15	09:30
8				
9				21:15
10	Week2	Start	End	Hours
11	Monday	09:30	18:30	09:00
12	Tuesday	10:15	19:15	09:00
13	Wednesday	09:30	18:15	08:45
14	Thursday	10:00	20:00	10:00
15	Friday	10:30	19:00	08:30
16				
17				
18				

6 As soon as both the 'Start' and 'End' times have been entered, Excel subtracts one from the other and a value will appear in the 'Hours' column. The total will be calculated automatically at the top of your spreadsheet. If you want to add more weeks to your sheet, copy the range from A1 to D7 and paste it at A9. Then delete the copy of the title. You can then add week numbers above the 'Monday' cells.

Recording a macro

Although all Excel's tools can be accessed with a few mouse clicks, you may find yourself performing some sequences of events again and again. This can be tedious, especially if you have to repeat them many times a day. Fortunately, Excel can store your actions as a series of commands, called a macro, ready to be played back automatically whenever you like.

SEE ALSO...
● *Print your work p 28*
● *Change menus and toolbars p 84*

BEFORE YOU START
Click on the **View** menu, choose **Toolbars** and then **Customize**. Click on the **Toolbars** tab, put a tick in the box next to 'Stop Recording' and then click on the **Close** button.

1 Highlight any area of data in a spreadsheet. Then click on the **Tools** menu, choose **Macro** then **Record New Macro**. Type a relevant name for your macro so you can easily recall its function later – we've called ours 'PrintSelection'. Then select 'Personal Macro Workbook' from the drop-down menu under **Store macro in**.

2 Click on the **OK** button. Excel is now recording all your mouse clicks and actions, so be careful to click the correct buttons and menu items. Make sure the **Relative Reference** button on the **Macro** toolbar is selected (light blue). Go to the **File** menu and choose **Print**. When the **Print** dialogue box opens, put a dot next to 'Selection' and click the **Preview** button. Then click on the **Close** button and click on the **Stop** button on the **Macro** toolbar. If the toolbar does not disappear, click on its **Close** button.

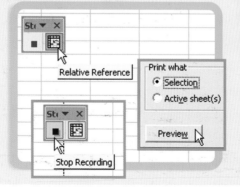

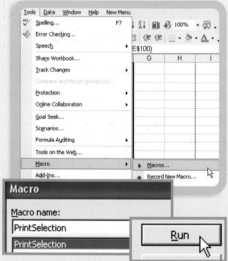

3 To check your macro, select an area of data, click on the **Tools** menu, select **Macro** and choose **Macros**. Then select your macro name and click on the **Run** button. Excel will immediately place the selected area on a page in the **Print Preview** window. Click the **Print** button to print or the **Close** button to return to the Excel window.

Absolute and relative macros

A macro can be either 'absolute' or 'relative'. An absolute macro operates on specific cells, regardless of which cell is selected when you start it. A relative macro runs relative to the selected cell. For example, if you recorded an absolute macro that started in cell B2 then selected cell B1 and made this cell bold, then whenever you ran that macro it would always make B1 bold, no matter which cell was selected when you ran it. However, a relative macro recording the same steps would always make the cell above the selected cell bold, because it would contain no reference to B1, just instructions to move up one cell and then apply bold formatting.

Expert advice

To create a menu for your macros, right-click the **Menu** bar and choose **Customize**. Click on **Commands** then on 'New Menu' under **Categories**. Drag 'New Menu' from the **Commands** list to your **Menu** bar. Then scroll to 'Macros' on the left and drag 'Custom Menu Item' over **New Menu** on the **Menu** bar and down to the empty square that appears. Click on **New Menu** and right-click on **Custom Menu Item** to assign a macro.

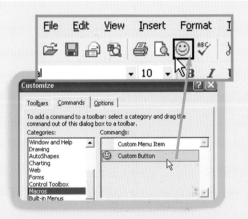

5 If you need to move the button, drag it to a new location. Once the button is in the correct place, right-click on it and choose **Assign Macro**. Then click on your new macro in the **Assign Macro** dialogue box and click on **OK**, followed by **Close**. Now, every time you click the smiley face, the selected area will be placed in the **Print Preview** window, ready for printing, and the last **Setup** settings will be applied.

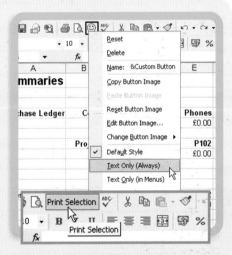

4 You can create a toolbar button for your macro so that you can activate it with a single click. Right-click anywhere on the **Standard** toolbar and choose **Customize** from the pop-up menu. Then click on the **Commands** tab and scroll down to 'Macros' in the **Categories** list on the left. From the **Commands** list on the right, click and drag the 'Custom Button' option onto your **Standard** toolbar and drop it where you'd like your new macro button to go.

6 To change the smiley face button to a more informative text button, right-click on any toolbar and choose **Customize** to open the **Customize** dialogue box. Then right-click on the smiley face and select **Text Only (Always)**. Right-click on the button again (which now reads **Custom Button**) and type 'Print Selection' next to **Name**. Then click the **Close** button in the **Customize** dialogue box.

Create a company ledger

Excel is ideal for monitoring personal expenditure and managing lists, but it is also powerful enough to make light work of business accounts and financial projections. Using multiple worksheets and Excel's AutoSum and SUMIF functions, it is possible to create a basic purchase and sales ledger to keep track of expenses incurred and sales made by a small company.

SEE ALSO...
- *Using AutoSum* p 26
- *Advanced functions* p 90

BEFORE YOU START
*Right-click on the Sheet 1 worksheet tab at the bottom of the Excel window, select **Rename** and type 'Purchase'. Name Sheet 2 'Sales' and Sheet 3 'Summary'.*

PURCHASE LEDGER

A purchase ledger keeps track of expenses incurred by your company in the course of its business.

1 Click in cell A1 and type 'Purchase Ledger'. Format the text as bold and change the font size to 14pt using the tools on the **Formatting** toolbar. In row 4, type the headings 'Date', 'Item', 'Code', Project', 'Amount', 'VAT', 'Paid by' and 'Notes'. Align the columns containing 'Project', 'Amount' and 'VAT' to the right and make all the headings bold.

2 Format the 'Amount' and 'VAT' columns as currency with a '£' symbol (see page 42). Then make the 'Item' and 'Notes' columns wider to allow space for text (see page 34). Select the 'Notes' column from the heading down and use the **Fill Color** palette to give it a light yellow background.

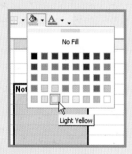

3 Add a dark border under your headings (see page 50). You can now add some data – type a date in column A and a description, such as 'Petrol', in column B. If you prefer to use a longer date style in the date column, click on the column header, then the **Format** menu, choose **Cells** and select the **Number** tab. Click on 'Date' under **Category** and then select '14 March 2001' under **Type**.

	A	B	C	D	E	F	G	H
1	**Purchase Ledger**							
2								
3					£34.50	£6.04		
4	**Date**	**Item**	**Code**	**Project**	**Amount**	**VAT**	**Paid by**	**Notes**
5	22 May 2003	Petrol	f		101	£25.50	£4.46	Chq	Trip to hardware store

The Name Box

Set up named areas so you can select areas quickly and easily, for instance to print or sort different sections of your data. Select the area you want to name and click in the **Name Box** to the left of the **Formula Bar**. Type a name and press **Return**. You can instantly return to this area by clicking the downward arrow in the name box and choosing your named area from the drop-down list.

Watch out

If you can't see a 'Sheet 3' tab, right-click on the **Sales** tab and choose **Insert**. Double-click on **Worksheet** and rename your new worksheet 'Summary'. Once you have a **Summary** tab, right-click on it and choose **Move or Copy**, then select **(move to end)** and click **OK**.

4 In column C we are going to allocate a single-letter code to each category of expenditure to enable Excel to work out how much you spent on each category. In this example, we use 'r' for rent, 'f' for fuel, 'p' for phone and 't' for tools.

In the 'Project' column, type a reference number for each project your company is undertaking so Excel can split your expenditure by project. In this example we will use 101–103.

For sundry items that are not related to any project, such as your office electricity bill, enter the letter 's'.

C	D	E
Code	**Project**	**Amount**
f	101	

5 The 'Paid by' column should contain an abbreviation that represents how the payment was made, such as 'Chq' for cheques, 'DD' for direct debit and 'CC' for credit card payments. This will enable you to check your accounts against your cheque book stubs and your bank and credit-card statements. Finally, you can add some informative notes to the 'Notes' column.

Paid by	Notes
Chq	Trip to hardware store
CC	To replace broken bits
DD	Ordering parts

=SUM(E5:E50)

Proj	SUM(number1, [number2], ...)		id
101	£25.50	£4.46	Chq
102	£7.50	£1.31	CC
103	£1.50	£0.26	DD
	£34.50	£6.04	
ject	**Amount**	**VAT**	Pai
101	£25.50	£4.46	Chc
102	£7.50	£1.31	CC

6 To total your 'Amount' column, click on cell E3 to select it. Then click on the **AutoSum** button, select cells E5 to E50 and press **Return**. Copy this function to F3 using the **Fill Handle** (see page 60, 'That's amazing!'). This totals your 'VAT' column. Then format cells E3 and F3 as bold.

Σ

SALES LEDGER

A sales ledger keeps track of all the sales your company has made. Since these amounts are based solely on the invoices your company issues, there is no need for a item code. However, we will still use the project codes so that income can be split by project on a summary sheet.

1 Click on the 'Sales' worksheet tab at the bottom of the Excel window. Type the title 'Sales Ledger' in cell A1 and then enter the column headings 'Date', 'Invoice num', 'Client', 'Project', 'Amount', 'VAT' and 'Notes' in row 4.

2 Format the title, your column headings and the cells in the same way as your purchase ledger (see page 98, steps 1–3). Now enter some data in the rows below. Use the 'Invoice Num' column for your invoice reference numbers, type the client's name in the 'Client' column and use the same project codes (101–103) in the 'Project' column. This means Excel will be able to split your invoiced amounts between projects on a summary sheet using its **SUMIF** function. Note that the amounts can be inclusive or exclusive of VAT, but this must match your purchase ledger (see 'That's amazing!' box below).

3 Add **AutoSum** totals above the headings 'Amount' and 'VAT' and make them stand out as before (see page 99, step 6).

	f_x =SUM(F5:F100)				
B	C	D	E	F	
			£1,125.00	£196.88	
e num	Client	Project	Amount	VAT No
123	S Jones	101	£1,000.00	£175.00 Fir:
124	J Smyth	102	£50.00	£8.75 Sm
125	C Mains	101	£75.00	£13.13 Se

	A	B	C	D	E	F	G
1	**Sales Ledger**						
2							
3					£1,125.00	£196.88	
4	**Date**	**Invoice num**	**Client**	**Project**	**Amount**	**VAT**	**Notes**
5	13 June 2003	123	S Jones	101	£1,000.00	£175.00	First of two invoices
6	29 June 2003	124	J Smyth	102	£50.00	£8.75	Small room
7	01 July 2003	125	C Mains	101	£75.00	£13.13	Second of two invoices
8							
9							
10							
11							
12							

Bright idea
Colour each worksheet tab to make it stand out. Right-click on the tab and choose Tab Color, *then select a colour from the pop-up palette and click on* OK.

That's amazing!
If you enter VAT inclusive amounts in your ledgers, Excel can extract the VAT for you. In the top cell of the VAT column just under the heading, type an '=' sign and click in the 'Amount' cell directly to its left. Then type '/1.175' and press **Return**. Excel will extract the VAT component of your sum. If you only have the VAT-exclusive figure, type '=', click in the 'Amount' cell and then type '/100*17.5' and press **Return**. Excel now works out the VAT at 17.5%.

SUMMARY SHEET

The summary worksheet will display breakdowns of your purchase and sales figures using Excel's SUMIF **function. This function will extract values from your purchase ledger and group them by item and project code.**

1 Select the 'Summary' worksheet tab, type 'Summary' in cell A1 and use the **Format Painter** button to copy the formatting from your purchase ledger title. In cell A4, type 'Purchase Ledger' and widen column A to fit the text. Starting in cell B4, type 'Code', 'Fuel', 'Rent', 'Phones' and 'Tools' across the row, align all but 'Code' to the right and make the whole row bold. Apply currency formatting to the cells under the headings (see page 98, step 2) and insert a heavy border as below.

2 Click on cell C5 and then on the **Insert Function** button. Select the 'Math & Trig' category and then choose 'SUMIF' from the list and click **OK**. This function totals amounts in a range that meet a specific criterion, such as 'f' for fuel, providing a breakdown of your expenditure by category.

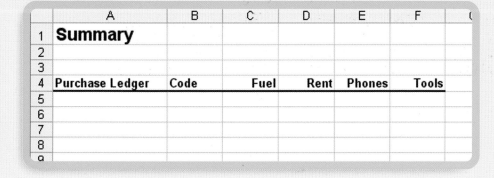

3 When the **Function Arguments** dialogue box appears, click on the **Collapse Dialogue** button (with the red arrow) to the right of the **Range** box. This opens a second **Function Arguments** box. Click the **Purchase** worksheet tab and select a range of cells from C5 to C50 and press **Return**.

Function Arguments

Purchase!C5:C50

Put '$' symbols before the 'C', '5', 'C' and '50' to create an absolute cell reference to the range C5 to C50. Then click in the **Criteria** box and type 'f'.

Click the **Collapse Dialogue** button to the right of the **Sum_range** box. Now switch to the purchase ledger worksheet by clicking the **Purchase** tab again. This time select cells E5 to E50 and press **Return**.

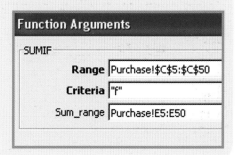

	A	B	C	D	E	F	
1	**Summary**						
2							
3							
4	**Purchase Ledger**	**Code**	**Fuel**	**Rent**	**Phones**	**Tools**	
5							
6							
7							
8							
9							

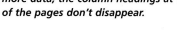

Close up
Remember to freeze your panes (see page 72) so that as you scroll down and enter more data, the column headings at the top of the pages don't disappear.

4 Add the '$' symbols as in step 3 and click the **OK** button. Excel now looks in the range C5 to C50 in your purchase ledger and adds together the amounts that have an 'f' (for Fuel) next to them in the 'Code'

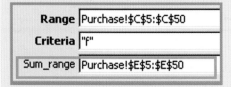

Range	Purchase!$C$5:$C$50
Criteria	"f"
Sum_range	Purchase!$E$5:$E$50

column. Copy this formula across to the range D5 to F5 on your summary worksheet using the **Fill Handle**. Carefully change the 'f' in each of the formulas to an 'r' to represent 'Rent', a 'p' for 'Phones' and a 't' for 'Tools'.

10	B	I	U					%	,			

✓ *fx* =SUMIF(Purchase!$C$5:$C$50,"t",Purchase!$E$5:$E$50)

SUMIF(range, **criteria**, [sum_range]) |E | F | G |

Code	Fuel	Rent	Phones	Tools
	£25.50	£25.50	£25.50	=SUMIF(P|

Excel now extracts and totals the 'Rent', 'Phones' and 'Tools' amounts. You can add extra codes for any other cost categories by copying the formula across and editing the code as above.

5 The same method can be used to extract and total the amounts by project. Select and copy the range B4 to F5 and paste at cell B7. Change the 'Code' heading to 'Project', 'Fuel' to 'Sundries', 'Rent' to 'P101', 'Phones' to 'P102' and 'Tools' to 'P103'.

SUMIF ▼ ✗ ✓ *fx* =SUMIF(Purchase!$D$5:$D$50,"s",Purchase!$E$5:$E$50)

A		SUMIF(range, **criteria**, [sum_range]) |E	F	G
1	**Summary**				
2					
3					
4	**Purchase Ledger**	Code	Fuel	Rent	Phones	Tools
5			£25.50	£0.00	£1.50	£7.50
6						
7		Project	Sundries	P101	P102	P103
8			$D$50,"s"|	£0.00	£1.50	£7.50
9						
10						
11						

SUMIF ▼ ✗ ✓ *fx* =SUMIF(Purchase!$D$5:$D$50,"103",Purchase!$E$5:$E$50)

A		SUMIF(range, **criteria**, [sum_range]) |E	F	G
1	**Summary**				
2					
3					
4	**Purchase Ledger**	Code	Fuel	Rent	Phones	Tools
5			£25.50	£0.00	£1.50	£7.50
6						
7		Project	Sundries	P101	P102	P103
8			£0.00	£25.50	£7.50	50,"103",P|
9						
10						
11						

The 'P's are inserted so we can make a chart (see page 103). Edit the formula in cell C8 so that all the 'C's become 'D's and the 'f' becomes an 's'. Then copy the formula to cells D8 through F8. Edit those cells so that the 's' becomes the codes '101', '102' or '103' respectively.

Use Find and Replace
If you want to change repeated text in a range of cells, you can use **Find and Replace** to make the changes automatically. Highlight the cells containing the data, click on the **Edit** menu and choose **Find and Replace**. Click on the **Options** button and select 'Formulas' under **Look in**. Then type the word you want to change next to **Find what** and the replacement word next to **Replace with** and click the **Replace All** button.

Bright idea
Add AutoFilters (see page 76) to your purchase and sales ledgers so you can isolate items and view them according to their code or project. For example, you can use two filters to view all project 101 purchases that fall into the tools category.

6 You also could set up a summary for your 'Sales' using the **SUMIF** formula. To do this, copy the 'Project' headings and formulas down a few rows and add a 'Sales' heading. Format these in the same way as before. Instead of your **SUMIF** formulas referring to the purchase ledger, they must refer to the sales ledger, so change the word 'Purchase' to 'Sales' in each of

=SUMIF(Sales!$D$5:$D$50,"s",Sales!$E$5:$E$50)

the formulas. Before you enter all your data, try adding just a few items into your purchase and sales ledgers. Start with one amount and test it by trying it with each code and then each project, checking the summary sheet each time to make sure it is extracting the values. Then try typing in more values to make sure Excel is totalling items correctly.

Purchase Ledger

				£34.50	£6.04		
Date	Item	Code	Project	Amount	VAT	Paid by	Notes
22 May 2003	Petrol	f	101	£25.50	£4.46	Chq	Trip to hardware store
23 May 2003	Drill bits	t	102	£7.50	£1.31	CC	To replace broken bits
01 June 2003	Calls to suppliers	p	103	£1.50	£0.26	DD	Ordering parts

Summary

Purchase Ledger	Code	Fuel	Rent	Phones	Tools
		£25.50	£0.00	£1.50	£7.50
	Project	Sundries	P101	P102	P103
		£0.00	£25.50	£7.50	£1.50
Sales Ledger	Project	Sundries	P101	P102	P103
		£0.00	£1,075.00	£50.00	£0.00

Purchase Ledger

				£34.50
Date	Item	Code	Project	Amount
22 May 2003	Petrol	f	101	£25.50
23 May 2003	Drill bits	t	102	£7.50
01 June 2003	Calls to suppliers	p	103	£1.50

Sales Ledger

				£1,125.00
Date	Invoice num	Client	Project	Amount
13 June 2003	123	S Jones	101	£1,000.00
29 June 2003	124	J Smyth	102	£50.00
01 July 2003	125	C Mains	101	£75.00

Add a chart
Add a chart to your summary worksheet to show how expenditure compares across projects or by category. Highlight the range from C11 to F12, click on the **Chart Wizard** button and click on **Finish**. Excel inserts a barchart. The reason that the cells are labelled 'P101' instead of '101' is that Excel will not recognise numbers as chart headings and will try to turn your project numbers into bars on the graph.

GLOSSARY

A

Active window The window in which you are working. To activate a window, click on it and it will position itself in front of any other open windows on screen.

Alignment The position of data in a cell. Data can be aligned to the left or right, top or bottom, or centred in the middle of the cell.

Alt key The key to the left of the Spacebar on the keyboard, which activates a command when pressed in combination with other keys. *See Shift key*.

Arrow keys The four keys at the bottom of the keyboard that move the insertion point up, down, left and right, and allow you to scroll through a list or menu.

AutoFill An Excel function that fills a series of cells with data based on the data in adjacent cells, such as days of the week, months or a series of numbers. It can also be used to copy formulas across a range of cells. *See Function and Fill Handle*.

AutoFormat A built-in range of formats that you can apply in one go to selected cells.

AutoShapes A selection of predesigned graphic shapes – from simple rectangles and circles to more complex arrows and stars – that you can insert in a spreadsheet and customise to suit your needs.

AutoSum An Excel function that adds up a series of values in a range of cells. *See Function*.

B

Background A colour, texture or image positioned on the spreadsheet as a layer, on top of which all other data and objects sit. Also the image on the Windows Desktop.

Backspace key This key, often showing a left-facing arrow, is located in the top right-hand corner of the main block of letter keys on the keyboard. It deletes data to the left of the insertion point. *See Delete key*.

Bitmap An on-screen image made up of tiny dots or pixels.

Bold A text format that makes the selected text appear heavier and darker for emphasis.

Browse To search through the contents of a computer, viewing the names of the files in each folder.

Button An on-screen image, that you click to perform a function, for example, clicking on the OK or Yes buttons in a dialogue box confirms an action.

C

Caps Lock Pressing this key will cause all letters that you type to appear as capitals (upper case). Press the key again to return to standard characters. *See Shift key*.

Cell A small, rectangular area in a spreadsheet, database or table, into which data or figures are entered. Click on a cell to select it. Each cell has a unique address made up of its column and row co-ordinates.

Chart A graphic representation of data, such as a graph, that can be inserted into an Excel spreadsheet.

Click To press and release the left mouse button once. Menu and dialogue box options and toolbar buttons are chosen, and ranges selected, in this way.

Clip Art Graphic images that come with Microsoft Office programs. These can be inserted into spreadsheets and then resized and manipulated.

Clipboard A virtual location where items that have been cut or copied from a spreadsheet are stored. The Office Clipboard can store 24 items of data at a time, regardless of their size. Use the Paste command on the Standard toolbar to insert the most recently copied or cut item in a spreadsheet. Use the Office Clipboard command on the Edit menu to view the entire Clipboard.

Close A command on the File menu to shut down the active window or spreadsheet, but not the program. It serves the same function as clicking the 'Close Window' button under the 'Close' button with a red cross.

Comment A small pop-up note attached to a cell, which only appears when the mouse pointer is hovering over the cell. Cells with comments attached have small red triangles in the top right corner.

Conditional formatting An Excel feature that applies cell and font formatting according to conditions fulfilled by the cell contents.

Copy To make a duplicate of a file or section of a spreadsheet and store it in the Clipboard. *See Clipboard*.

Criteria A set of conditions specified by the user, by which data is searched and matching results are identified.

Cursor A marker, usually a flashing vertical line, which appears when you are entering or editing data in a cell. Also called the 'insertion point'.

Cursor keys *See Arrow keys*.

Cut To remove selected data and/or images to the Clipboard, where they are stored for later use. In Excel, cut objects are not removed from the spreadsheet until they are pasted.

D

Default The manufacturer's settings for a program that are in effect when no others have been specified by the user.

Delete To completely remove a selected file or folder from your hard disk, or some data or a range of cells from your spreadsheet.

Delete key This is located in the group of six keys to the right of the main block of letter keys on the keyboard. This key deletes data to the right of the insertion point. *See Backspace key*.

Desktop The background screen on your PC. It is the starting point for all work.

Dialogue box A window that appears on screen when you are using a program. It asks for further instructions to be input by the user in order to complete a procedure.

Double-click To press and release the left mouse button twice in quick succession. This is most often used to open spreadsheets from within folders, to open folders and to activate programs.

Drag A mouse action used to highlight data, to reshape objects, to move an object or file and to select a range of cells. Click and keep the left button held down, then move the mouse as required.

Drawing toolbar A supplementary toolbar shared across all Office programs, which contains options for adding graphic elements to your Excel spreadsheets.

Drop-down menu A list of options that appears when you click on one of the headings on the Menu bar or when you click on a small downward arrow next to a list item. Move down the list and click once on an item to select it.

E

End Using this key in conjunction with the arrow keys enables you to quickly hop up or down to the next filled cell, or to the left or right end of a row of filled cells.

Error message A small window on screen, warning that a fault has occurred and, where possible, suggesting an action to remedy it.

F

File Any item stored on a computer's hard disk, whether it is a program, a spreadsheet, or an image.

File extension A three or four-letter code, also known as a suffix, at the end of a filename. It states the file type, so Windows knows which program to use to open it.

File format The way in which files created by different programs are saved. *See File extension.*

Fill To apply a chosen colour to a selected range of cells or to an object, such as a square or chart. You can also apply a mix of colours using 'Fill Effects'.

Fill Handle A small square at the bottom right corner of a cell, which, when clicked on and dragged to adjacent cells, performs an AutoFill. *See AutoFill.*

Filter To isolate certain items from a list according to a specified criterion or criteria. For example, to display only those items over £100 or which match a word, such as 'Gas'. *See List.*

Folder A virtual storage location on the PC's hard disk, designed to help you keep related files and relevant spreadsheets together.

Font A specific style and set of characters for a typeface, such as Times New Roman.

Footer An area at the base of every page of a spreadsheet that contains information relevant to the whole spreadsheet, such as page numbers. Footers are only visible in Print Preview mode. *See Header.*

Form A dialogue box that provides an easy way to enter or display data in the rows of an Excel database.

Format To alter your data's appearance by applying style, number and colour options.

Formula A set of conditions that carry out a mathematical calculation.

Formula Bar The area at the top of the Excel screen below the toolbars, where you can view and edit the contents of cells.

Freeze panes To fix an area of a spreadsheet so that the headings at the top or left of the screen are visible even when you have scrolled down or across the page.

Function A preset formula built in to Excel, such as 'SUMIF'.

Function keys The 12 'F' keys at the top of the computer keyboard, ranging from F1 to F12, some of which perform special tasks.

G

Gradient A fill effect that fills an area or an object starting with one colour and ending with another.

Graphic Any type of digital image on a computer, including Clip Art, photographs and illustrations.

H

Handle The small squares that appear at the corners and sides of an object when you select it. They allow you to adjust the dimensions of the object by dragging them to a different position.

Hard disk A magnetic storage device in a computer, which retains its data when the computer is turned off.

Header An area at the top of each page of a spreadsheet, which can contain information, such as the title. Headers are not visible on your spreadsheet unless you select Print Preview mode. *See Footer.*

Help key Usually the F1 key on the keyboard. This key accesses a program's built-in Help database, which gives advice on performing a task. *See Function keys.*

Home Pressing this key takes you to column A (the first column) in the currently selected row.

I

Icon A graphical representation of a program, file or a function, designed to be easily recognisable. Double-click on icons to launch them.

Insert To add an element to a spreadsheet, such as an image or new rows or columns. This is usually done using the Insert menu.

Insertion point *See Cursor.*

Italic A style of typeface whereby the letters are displayed and printed with a slight slant to the right.

K

Keyboard shortcut A combination of keys pressed simultaneously to issue a specific command.

L

Landscape A printing mode that prints a page orientated with the longest side running across the page rather than down. *See Portrait.*

List A series of data entered in columns of similar items. Also, a series of options under a heading in a dialogue box.

M

Macro A series of commands or actions that are recorded and can be played back when triggered by a menu selection, button or keystroke.

Margins The white space around the edge of a printed spreadsheet area, the dimensions of which can be adjusted.

Maximize To increase the size of a program or folder window so that it covers the entire Windows Desktop area except the Taskbar.

Menu bar A toolbar at the top of a program window containing text headings which, when clicked, display categorised options in drop-down menus.

Merge To combine two or more cells into one cell that is the same height or width as the space previously occupied by the cells selected for the merge.

Minimize To reduce a window to a button on the Taskbar. This allows you to continue running several programs without cluttering the Desktop with windows.

Mouse pointer A small arrow or cursor on screen that moves in relation to the mouse. In Excel, the pointer changes depending on whether you are working with cells, menus or drawings.

My Documents A special folder designed to store files created by the user.

N

Normal The default view that appears when you open a spreadsheet.

Nudge A menu command that moves the selected object a small amount in a chosen direction. This is useful for aligning drawing objects.

O

Object An item, such as a square, circle, arrow, image or file, created in another program, which can be inserted into a spreadsheet and modified at any time.

Office Assistant An animated character who offers help as you work in Excel. The assistant can be switched on and off, and its settings can be altered to suit the way you work. Click anywhere on the Assistant to open a small window where you can type your questions.

Open To bring a file, folder or program into use. This action loads the file's data from the PC's hard disk into its memory (RAM).

Orientation An option available when printing a spreadsheet. Users can choose to set up the page as either Landscape (of greater width than height) or Portrait (of greater height than width), depending on how they want the data to appear. *See Landscape and Portrait.*

P

Page break The column or row in a spreadsheet at which one page ends and another begins when it is printed. Page breaks can be set up manually if necessary.

Page Setup The settings that allow you to specify the layout of your page, margin sizes, paper size and how your spreadsheet prints. This section also includes tools for adding headers and footers.

Page Up/Page Down These keys take you up or down your spreadsheet respectively, by one screen at a time.

Paste To insert text or other data that has been cut or copied to the Office Clipboard into a spreadsheet.

Paste Special Options that enable you to choose exactly how you want data to be pasted. For example, you can paste formats only, or just the results of formulas.

Places bar A strip at the left-hand side of an Office program's Open and Save As dialogue boxes, which offers shortcuts to commonly accessed locations. You can also add your own locations to this bar.

Point size A standard scale for measuring typefaces. For example, the text on this page is 8 point, whereas large newspaper headlines are often 72 point.

Pop-up menu A list of options that appears when you right-click on an object. Also called a context menu.

Portrait A printing mode which prints with the shortest side of a page running along the top. *See Landscape.*

Print Preview The on-screen display of how a spreadsheet will look on the page when it is printed. Changes cannot be made to the spreadsheet when using Print Preview mode.

R

Radio button A small white circle beside an option, which you click on to activate or deactivate the option. An activated option will have a black dot in the radio button. It is not possible to select more than one radio button under one heading.

Range A group of adjacent cells in a table or spreadsheet. A range in Excel has a start cell address and an end address, for example, A1 to D3 (written in Excel formulas as 'A1:D3').

Redo (Repeat) To repeat the last action. This can be used to speed up repeated tasks or to reapply an action you have just undone. *See Undo.*

Resize To adjust the dimensions of an object, such as a chart, square or circle, drawn in an Excel document. Do this by clicking and dragging the handles (small black boxes) that appear around an object's edges when it is selected.

Return key The large key on the right-hand side of the main block of keys on the keyboard. Press it to confirm data entry or editing.

Right-click To press and release the right mouse button once.

S

Save To copy the current spreadsheet from memory to the hard disk. The first time you choose Save, the Save As box opens to allow you to choose a name for your file. Once you have chosen a name, Save uses the selected name and location automatically. *See Save As.*

Save As This function allows you to allocate a new name to a file you have already saved. It also lets you save an existing spreadsheet in a different location or in an alternative format without affecting the original saved file.

Scaling To resize the data in the print area to fit the page. You can choose a percentage or fit the data to a specified number of pages. Scaling does not affect the data in the spreadsheet, it simply changes the way it is printed.

Scroll To move through the contents of a window or a drop-down list, either vertically or horizontally.

Scroll bar The narrow strips running down the right-hand side and along the bottom of a window. By clicking and dragging the block along the panel you can quickly scroll down the page or from side to side. Use the small arrows at the end of either scroll bar to move around slowly.

Search A Windows program that searches for a file, usually by its name or creation date. From within Excel you can use Search to scan your hard disk for files that contain specific information, such as a word or phrase.

Select To click on a cell or to click and drag over a range of cells so that they are highlighted. A cell is also selected when you move to it using the keyboard cursor keys.

Shift key This serves various functions. It can be used to type a capital letter when pressed at the same time as a letter, or to access the symbols on the number keys.

Sort An Excel feature that organises data in a list. Excel can sort by multiple criteria, such as numerically by 'Date' and also alphabetically by 'Name' or 'Description'.

Spacebar The wide key positioned in the centre at the bottom of the keyboard that is used to insert spaces between words.

Splash screen A panel that appears briefly while a program is being loaded, giving details of the program's creators and version.

Split To divide the Excel window into separate areas, each of which can display a different area of your spreadsheet.

Spreadsheet A document for storing and calculating numerical data and text. A spreadsheet is made up of a grid of cells, arranged in columns and rows, into which data is entered. Excel's spreadsheets are known as worksheets. *See Worksheet*.

Standard toolbar The line of small icons that sits at the top of the window, and which contains common commands used when creating spreadsheet documents. These include Save, Print, Cut, Copy and Paste.

Status bar The bar running along the bottom of program windows containing information about the current spreadsheet.

Style The appearance of the various elements of a spreadsheet. Excel allows you to define 'Styles', which enable you to apply a range of formats in one go. *See Format*.

T

Tab Short for 'tabulate'. In a spreadsheet, this key moves you one cell to the right. *See Tab key*.

Tab key The key to the left of the 'Q' key, used to move between cells in spreadsheets, or between fields in a form. *See Form*.

Task Pane An optional panel at the right of Excel's window, which provides quick access to frequently used features, such as Clip Art, and recently accessed documents.

Taskbar The strip, usually positioned along the bottom of the Windows Desktop, that displays the Start button, small Quick Launch icons for starting programs, and large buttons for any programs and documents that are currently open.

Template A format for saving a spreadsheet so that its elements can be used as the basis for similar spreadsheets. Some templates are supplied with Excel and are available from the Task Pane. If you save a file as a Template, it will appear in the General Templates section.

Texture A type of fill effect that uses built-in images or a specified image file as a fill for an object.

Tick box A square white box next to an option in a dialogue box that, when clicked, displays a tick to signify it is selected.

Toolbar A bar or window containing buttons and drop-down lists for issuing commands or functions.

Typeface *See Font*.

U

Undo A function that allows you to reverse the last task or series of tasks that you carried out.

V

View A menu of options which allows you to change the way a spreadsheet is shown on screen and display certain toolbars.

W

Window The self-contained viewing and work area of a file, folder or program. Several windows can be open at once on the Desktop. A program can have several windows, each for an open file.

Wizard A program tool that guides users step by step through a series of tasks.

WordArt Text created in a graphic form that can be inserted into a spreadsheet for decorative effect.

Workbook An Excel document is called a workbook and can contain multiple spreadsheets, called worksheets. *See Worksheet*.

Worksheet Individual spreadsheets within an Excel workbook, accessed by clicking the tabs at the bottom of the screen. *See Workbook*.

Wrap The way text flows within a cell. Wrapped text will not overflow the right side of the cell but is forced to a new line, expanding the cell downwards to make room.

Z

Zoom To enlarge an area of a spreadsheet for ease of viewing.

INDEX

Numbers shown in **bold** type represent the main references to the subject listed.

Acknowledgments

We would like to thank the following individuals and
organisations for their assistance in producing this book.

Photography: John Freeman

Software: Microsoft Press Office